TEACHING
for
LEARNING
SUCCESS

Revised Edition

The Complete Handbook for
Classroom Organization and Management

by Gloria Frender

Incentive Publications, Inc.
Nashville, Tennessee

Cover by Rebecca Rüegger
Illustrated by Marta Drayton
Edited by Patience Camplair

ISBN 0-86530-636-2

1   2   3   4   5   6   7   8   9   10   07   06   05   04

PRINTED IN THE UNITED STATES OF AMERICA
www.incentivepublications.com

A Personal Note . . .

My first year of teaching was 1970. My first year of *learning* to teach was also 1970! College preparation gave me theory and nine weeks of practice teaching. Students gave me reality training and a love for sharing information.

I've learned from other teachers along the way, too, both what to do and what not to do.

It takes time, practice, and experience with the right skills and tools to strive for excellence and to inspire others. Every year of teaching needs to be a year of learning, because you can't do one without the other. Great teachers pass these skills and tools along to their students by *teaching* them the love for *learning*.

And so, I offer this book to you. It's a practical guide to use for your first—or twenty-first—year of teaching. Time and students have helped me mold the ideas within this book and have proven them highly successful. I'd like to share them with you because I believe in *Teaching for Learning Success*.

Gloria Frender
Boulder, Colorado 2004

The mediocre teacher tells.

The good teacher explains.

The superior teacher demonstrates.

The great teacher inspires.

—William Arthur Ward

Dedication

To Dean, my husband: Thank you for all your years of support, patience, encouragement, tolerance, listening, and understanding while I was grading, planning, phoning, meeting, teaching, learning, and writing.

To Kim and Kevin, our children: Thank you for sharing your opinions and ideas, giving wonderful advice, providing reality training, and understanding the frustrations and joys of a teacher and parent. I'm grateful and very proud to have been your first teacher.

To Nylene and Clark Collier, my parents: Thank you for being such wonderful first teachers. I have tried to pass on to our children what you shared with me.

To Spoof, a beloved cat: Thank you for warming my lap all those years while I was grading papers.

Acknowledgments

To Clara Balcom, a dear friend and great teacher, who inspired many, including me; to all my students over the past thirty-four years who have taught me and still keep in touch.

TABLE OF CONTENTS

Getting Set for Classroom Learning Success

ORGANIZING YOURSELF

PERSONAL ORGANIZATION

POLICY DECISIONS

LEARNING STYLES

CREATIVE TEACHING

LESSON PLANS

PREPARING FOR A SUBSTITUTE

ORGANIZING ENRICHMENT MATERIALS

GRADES

GIVING DIRECTIONS

✍ *Indicates ready-to-use forms or handouts*

Focus On Student Success

ABOUT THIS BOOK

This book was written by an experienced, practical, busy teacher and parent for all who want wonderful ideas, ready-made forms, and information at their fingertips. It focuses on practical success-building skills, tools, and materials ready for immediate use in any classroom or home.

If you are new to teaching, a seasoned educator, or somewhere in between, the topics discussed in *Teaching for Learning Success* will answer your questions and provoke further thought about teaching techniques. This resource offers an in-depth look at subjects essential to the classroom, including:

- teaching to students with various learning styles
- teacher, classroom, student organization and management skills and strategies
- school-home connections for better communication, more parental involvement, and increased student learning
- numerous cross-content and interdisciplinary skills and materials for teaching to students of all abilities in the classroom
- note-taking, review, and focusing techniques
- positive reinforcement and motivational games

Each section incorporates reproducible forms that can be used as overhead transparencies, student handouts, or tips for parents. You will find organizational checklists for students and teachers, sample planning outlines, hints for parents who want to help their children learn more effectively, a teacher evaluation, and learning tools such as graphic organizers.

Sure to spark new ideas and packed with useful tips and tools, *Teaching for Learning Success* is a practical guide you can turn to again and again.

ORGANIZING YOURSELF

✍ *Indicates ready-to-use forms or handouts*

ORGANIZING YOURSELF:

An Overview

Being organized is one of the best gifts you can give yourself. Why? Because it lowers stress, saves time and energy, strengthens your efforts and talents, and minimizes hassles. Organization plays an extremely vital role in teaching and can make your job infinitely easier. When you organize yourself, you also organize your teaching and your students.

This chapter contains complete plans for excellent personal and professional organizational skills. The pages are designed to be reproduced and used immediately. These checklists, forms, and ideas will make your job easier, from those days of preparation before students arrive to checking in your keys at the end of the year.

BEGINNING-OF-THE-YEAR & END-OF-THE-YEAR CHECKLISTS

Here are two checklists that will help you organize yourself for a terrific school year!

Use the comprehensive checklist on pages 16 and 17 before school begins. Your time is precious, and you need to make the most of it—this timesaver is organized into six categories:

- ◆ Teacher's Desk Items

- ◆ Personal Items

- ◆ Teacher References

- ◆ File Cabinet

- ◆ Handouts to Reproduce

- ◆ To Do Before Students Arrive

Begin by making a copy of this list and checking off each item or task as you complete it. Cross off any items that do not pertain to you and add any that are not included. It's that simple.

Finish the school year by completing the "End-of-the-Year Checklist" on page 18. Remember, being organized saves you time, money, energy, effort, and stress!

BEGINNING-OF-THE-YEAR CHECKLIST

Teacher's Desk Items: (*Consider carefully the items you choose to place on top of your desk if your students will have access to them.*)

- [ ] pencils/erasers
- [ ] pens (black/blue ink)
- [ ] correcting pens (try green; let students use red)
- [ ] dry-erase pens and erasers
- [ ] overhead transparency pens
- [ ] rulers
- [ ] paper clips (large and small)
- [ ] paper clamps (for sets of papers)
- [ ] clear tape
- [ ] masking tape
- [ ] straight pins
- [ ] push pins
- [ ] rubber tip fingers (for compiling handouts into packets)
- [ ] rubber bands (assorted sizes)
- [ ] stapler and staples
- [ ] staple remover
- [ ] facial tissue
- [ ] plastic, colored tabs (for use on 3-ring binder divider pages)
- [ ] index cards, in assorted sizes and colors
- [ ] index card file and alphabetical dividers (for student inventory cards)

- [ ] envelopes (assorted sizes)
- [ ] school stationery
- [ ] blank cards and envelopes to use as thank-you cards, etc.
- [ ] inexpensive bud vase or small flower base
- [ ] file folders and labels in various colors
- [ ] stackable paper organizer (to set on top of desk to hold file folders containing seating charts, etc.)
- [ ] notebook paper, unlined white scratch paper, and assorted colored paper
- [ ] first aid kit (usually distributed by the school's nurse's office)
- [ ] list of staff members and their classroom numbers
- [ ] building floor plan
- [ ] binder for substitutes (see pages 71–77)

Add Your Own:
- [ ] _____
- [ ] _____
- [ ] _____
- [ ] _____
- [ ] _____
- [ ] _____

Personal Items: (*Place in a secure drawer in your desk or a file cabinet.*)

- [ ] water bottle
- [ ] any medications (in case you forget to bring them from home)
- [ ] cough drops, sore throat lozenges
- [ ] nail clipper, emery board
- [ ] comb/brush
- [ ] eye care items (contact solution, extra contact or glasses case, glass cleaner, etc.)
- [ ] cosmetics (mirror, chapstick, lipstick, hand cream, etc.)

- [ ] snack items (paper cups, mug, crackers, cookies, tea bags, coffee, etc.)
- [ ] electric hot pot or coffee pot

Add Your Own:
- [ ] _____
- [ ] _____
- [ ] _____
- [ ] _____
- [ ] _____

Teacher References: (*Organize in an easily seen and accessible place for both you and substitutes.*)

- [ ] *Writers, Inc.* or *Write Source 2000* (see page 295)
- [ ] dictionary
- [ ] thesaurus
- [ ] almanac, atlas
- [ ] book of quotations
- [ ] general and specific reference materials for your curriculum
- [ ] binder containing school/district policies, union agreements, etc.

- [ ] binder containing multimedia ordering information and forms
- [ ] binder for cross-reference listing of your enrichment materials (see pages 78–81)

Add Your Own:
- [ ] _____
- [ ] _____
- [ ] _____
- [ ] _____
- [ ] _____

File Cabinet:

- ☐ labeled folders of handouts for Switch game (see pages 287–288)
- ☐ extra file folders
- ☐ files for general class preparation, organized in chronological order (grading system, vouchers, back-to-school night forms, etc.)
- ☐ labeled folder of transparency "sponges"

- ☐ bulletin board materials

  Add Your Own:
- ☐ _____
- ☐ _____
- ☐ _____
- ☐ _____
- ☐ _____

Handouts to Reproduce: *(Be sure you copy the appropriate items and amount for every class you teach. Label and file in correct locations, or place in binders.)*

- ☐ classroom rules
- ☐ syllabus for each class, as needed
- ☐ seating chart (see page 142)
- ☐ parent letter containing necessary policies, grading system, etc. (see pages 179–180)
- ☐ student explanation and grade sheet (see pages 161–163)
- ☐ class directory/study group inventory sheet (see page 158)
- ☐ vouchers (see pages 173–174)
- ☐ daily log explanation and daily log sheet for binder (see pages 139–140)
- ☐ parent/student phone log (see pages 192–193)
- ☐ blank calendar pages for students (see page 135)
- ☐ textbook checkout list (see page 148)
- ☐ teacher's daily "to do" list (see page 20) and calendar (see page 22)

- ☐ general information for the substitute form (see pages 74–75), daily lesson plan form (see page 76), and backup lesson plan form (see page 77)
- ☐ student honor award form (see page 279), super student award form (see page 280)
- ☐ appropriate pretests for each class
- ☐ student assignment sheet (see page 136)
- ☐ science lab report (see page 260)
- ☐ unit lesson plan form (see page 65)
- ☐ student response sheet (see page 223)
- ☐ vocabulary form (see page 250)
- ☐ weekly review forms (see pages 253–254)

  Add Your Own:
- ☐ _____
- ☐ _____
- ☐ _____
- ☐ _____
- ☐ _____

To Do Before Students Arrive:

Obtain appropriate keys for:
- ☐ classroom door(s)
- ☐ office
- ☐ file cabinet(s)
- ☐ production room
- ☐ media center
- ☐ computer lab

  Add Your Own:
- ☐ _____
- ☐ _____
- ☐ _____
- ☐ _____

- ☐ Pick up classroom enrollment lists; check with counselors for any students on your lists that might need immediate attention or special assistance.
- ☐ Read any student files concerning health limitations, learning disabled students, etc.
- ☐ Secure and organize textbooks for all classes.
- ☐ Arrange student desks, tables, lab tables, etc. (see pages 116–120).
- ☐ Set up a small table in the front of your room to serve as a potpourri table (see page 146).
- ☐ Supply teacher's desk with necessary materials.
- ☐ Copy all handouts to be distributed during the first week of school.

- ☐ Complete as much as possible of the substitute teacher folder (see pages 71–77).
- ☐ Complete a backup lesson plan for all classes (see page 77).
- ☐ Complete your first unit lesson plan (see pages 50–70).
- ☐ Fill in gradebook, with the exception of student names (see pages 82–85).
- ☐ Arrange bulletin boards (see pages 143–145).
- ☐ Secure necessary lab equipment.
- ☐ Write the first day's agenda on the chalkboard.
- ☐ Arrange necessary handouts in stacks in chronological order for each class.

  Add Your Own:
- ☐ _____
- ☐ _____
- ☐ _____
- ☐ _____
- ☐ _____
- ☐ _____

END-OF-THE-YEAR CHECKLIST

☐ Turn in all grade or scan sheets.

☐ Order supplies for next year (consumable student items, teacher references, teacher resources, enrichment materials, etc.).

☐ Cover bulletin boards with butcher paper to protect against fading from exposure to the sun and damage due to work crews.

☐ Send thank-you notes to volunteers, student assistants, etc.

☐ Secure desks and file cabinets.

☐ Secure textbooks (note text assignment numbers, quantities, etc.).

☐ Turn in student fines list (for damaged textbooks, missing library and reference books, etc.).

☐ Label appropriate boxes and stored material with your name and room number so that they will be returned to your room if they should be moved by work crews. (Secure tops with strong packing tape.)

☐ If you are moving to a different room, label everything and secure box lids with strong packing tape.

☐ Secure all game boxes, etc., with lids to keep out dust.

☐ Order textbooks for next year.

☐ Replace teacher's desk supplies.

☐ Cover bookshelves with butcher paper to keep from becoming too dusty.

☐ Organize and take home all materials appropriate for additional planning of future units, lessons, etc.

☐ Research possible grant monies to complete forms over the summer.

☐ Take home all plants, animals, and supplies.

☐ Find a vacation home for pets.

☐ Turn in appropriate keys.

☐ Complete all end-of-year paperwork for the principal.

☐ Write a brief description of your grading system, attach it to your gradebook or computer disk, and turn it into the administrative office. (If a question concerning final grades occurs, and you are unavailable, your principal will be able to answer it.)

☐ Obtain appropriate signatures from department chairman, librarian, office secretary, etc., if required for final checkout.

Add Your Own:

☐ _____
☐ _____
☐ _____
☐ _____
☐ _____
☐ _____
☐ _____
☐ _____
☐ _____
☐ _____
☐ _____
☐ _____
☐ _____
☐ _____
☐ _____

DAILY ORGANIZATION

It takes very little time to make time!

Making a "to do" list can save you not only time but energy, effort, and embarrassment—plus, it is easy to do. Simply think of what must be accomplished, organize your priorities hourly from morning to night, write them down, and mark them off when completed. You will be less likely to forget and more likely to complete tasks if you jot them down in an organized manner. The forms on the following pages are intended to be reproduced again and again to help you become more successful in making the best use of your time. Don't forget to add a few activities you want to do as rewards!

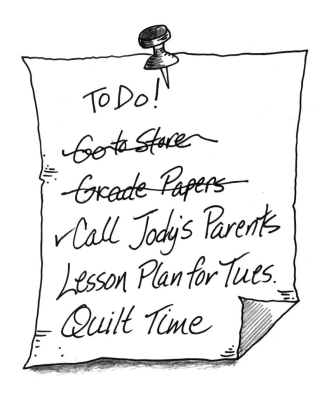

Experts tell us we are ten times more likely to complete a task if we take the time to write it down. You may want to pass along this tip to your students! (See pages 53-55, Learning to Learn, Rev. Ed. by Gloria Frender. Nashville, TN: Incentive Publications, 2004.)

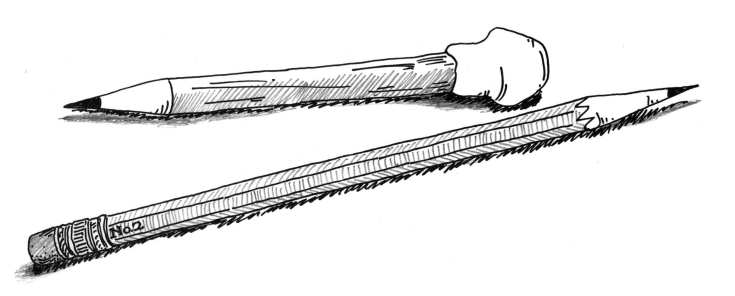

DAILY "TO DO" LIST

Day_____ Date_____ Name_____

TO DO

1. _____
2. _____
3. _____
4. _____
5. _____
6. _____
7. _____
8. _____
9. _____
10. _____
11. _____
12. _____
13. _____
14. _____
15. _____

TO CALL

Name	Phone #
_____	_____
_____	_____
_____	_____
_____	_____
_____	_____

TO CONTACT

_____

_____

_____

_____

_____

_____

_____

TO COPY

Item	Page #	# copies
1. _____	_____	_____
2. _____	_____	_____
3. _____	_____	_____
4. _____	_____	_____
5. _____	_____	_____

TO TAKE HOME

_____

_____

_____

_____

_____

NOTES: _____

_____

_____

_____

_____

Teaching for Learning Success, Rev. Ed.

WEEKLY CALENDAR

Month _____   Week _____

Name _____   Period _____

Teacher _____

Sunday
Monday
Tuesday
Wednesday
Thursday
Friday
Saturday
Notes:

DAILY CALENDAR

Month _____ Week _____

Name _____ Period _____

Teacher _____

7:00 AM 7:30 AM	
8:00 AM 8:30 AM	
9:00 AM 9:30 AM	
10:00 AM 10:30 AM	
11:00 AM 11:30 AM	
12:00 PM 12:30 PM	
1:00 PM 1:30 PM	
2:00 PM 2:30 PM	
3:00 PM 3:30 PM	
4:00 PM 4:30 PM	
5:00 PM 5:30 PM	
6:00 PM 6:30 PM	
Notes:	

Teaching for Learning Success, Rev. Ed.

MAKING CLASSROOM POLICY DECISIONS

Deciding on your classroom policy is never an easy task. It is much more difficult, however, to begin teaching with no policy at all. A classroom policy decision made in haste and without any forethought could turn out to be a serious mistake. Think carefully about how you want to run your classroom, and then develop a set of rules you can enforce fairly and with which you can live comfortably.

There will always be district, school, departmental, or team rules that will affect your classroom policy. Be sure that you understand all of them. You may also want to review other teachers' policies if they will affect your class. A close examination of the ways in which other teachers run their classrooms can also help you develop ideas of your own.

Think about these questions as you are making your decisions. After you have formed your policy on a particular issue, apply them to each decision.

1. Does my policy conflict with existing school/district policies?

2. Is my policy realistic?

3. Is my policy fair and consistent for all students?

4. Can I enforce my policy fairly and easily?

5. Am I comfortable with my policy?

6. Does my policy reinforce a good learning atmosphere?

7. Does my policy teach students to become successful, independent students?

8. Is my policy consistent with my overall teaching philosophy?

9. Will my policy make my job teaching easier or more difficult?

Now you are ready to tackle some policy decisions on your own! Keep them simple and short. Don't be afraid to modify or change your decisions as needed, but do so sparingly. If you do alter your policy, make it a point to notify (preferably in writing) anyone affected by the change, and allow some time before your new policy goes into effect.

After you have made your list of classroom policies, prepare a handout for distribution to each student the first day of the year or course. Be sure to include the course title and grade level, your name and contact information, a brief statement of your goals, a course description, the titles of materials used, a list of classroom rules with your absence/tardiness and grading policies, and your discipline system. Make two copies, one for parents and the other to keep for your files. Require parents and students to sign and return these statements.

MAKING CLASSROOM POLICY DECISIONS

Consider the following situations before you begin (check building and district rules):

1. level of expectation for student achievement and behavior

2. grading system (point system, letter grades, weighted grades, assigned percentages for homework, tests, and participation, rounding up grades, etc.)

3. late assignments

4. papers with no names

5. amount of student involvement in lesson planning, grading papers in class, assembling bulletin boards, policy making, grading guidelines, teacher evaluations

6. allowing gum, food, beverages, hats, etc., in the classroom

7. persistent tardies

8. giving out your home phone number and encouraging students to call you

9. staying after school on a regular basis to tutor students

10. setting office hours

11. students leaving during class and acceptable reasons for doing so

12. students leaving class once it has begun to retrieve work from their lockers, etc.

13. students leaving class during tests

14. students who do not complete tests and want more time to work later in the day

15. when papers are due in class (at the beginning of class or by the end of class)

16. when it is best to remove students from the classroom because of negative behavior

17. students looking at their grades in your gradebook

18. use of unacceptable language

19. students taking back papers after they are turned in

20. where students should be at the beginning of class

21. expected student behavior when you are called out of the room

22. students losing handouts and wanting you to copy additional ones for them

23. negative student behavior directed toward a substitute teacher

24. making up missed tests

25. paraprofessional aids, student assistants, parent volunteers, etc., entering grades in the gradebook or on a computer

26. students who come to class unprepared (with no paper, pen or pencil, book, etc.)

Teaching for Learning Success, Rev. Ed.

CLASSROOM POLICY DECISIONS:
———— Realistic and Valuable Suggestions ————

When making policy decisions you will need to take into account district and building policies, as well as the age and maturity level of students. Other factors such as learning disabilities and mental capabilities will also greatly affect policy decisions. Read through the following suggestions, selecting any you feel would work for you. Modify or adjust them to fit your particular teaching style and situation.

> *Author's note: These policies merely reflect personal standards and have proven highly successful in my classrooms. They have also been well received by students, parents, and administrators.*

1. What is your level of expectation for student achievement and behavior?

Students will rise to your expectations, provided they are realistic and fair—so why not have high ones? Use this phrase with students: "I have faith in you. I really think you can do this!" If you say this sincerely, you will be amazed at how much students can accomplish. This promotes self-reliance and self-esteem.

2. What is your grading system (point system, letter grades, weighted grades, assigned percentages for homework, tests, and participation, rounding up grades, etc.)?

A true point system provides the most accurate method of formulating grades and also simplifies your work when adding extra credit or participation points to a student's overall grade. When rounding up a student's grade, use .5 as a marker. For example, if a student's grades average to 89.4, the overall grade will remain a B+. A grade of 89.8 is rounded up to an A- (if the grading scale is 90–100 = A, 80–89 = B, etc.). When calculating final grades, also consider placing more emphasis on daily work, as it provides a better overall representation of a student's efforts than does one test given on a particular day. Consider calculating overall grades using this formula:

daily work = 50%
tests and quizzes = 30%
participation and attitude = 15%
extra credit = 5%

Consider establishing a policy to deal with students who earn all passing grades but complete only 50% of the total assignments. One method of handling such a situation is to require that a minimum of 60% of all assignments, quizzes, and tests must be turned in in order to pass the course, regardless of a student's overall grade. Keep in mind that students earn grades; you only correct their work.

Extra credit points are popular among students and often motivate them if the extra credit assignments are appropriate and fun. When reviewing the grading policy with students, state clearly, both in writing and in discussion, the policy on extra credit work. consider setting a limit on the total amount of extra credit points a student can earn, so that extra credit points can only slightly affect a student's overall grade. It is also a good idea to establish a plan to deal with a student who lets his or her work suffer all semester and then requests a large amount of extra credit work in order to rescue his or her failing grade. It is not the purpose of extra credit assignments to raise a failing grade: students should complete all of the work assigned for each course.

3. What is your policy regarding late assignments?

Many teachers accept late assignments but take off a certain amount of points for each day the assignment is late. If you choose to do this, keep in mind that keeping track of the necessary paperwork can become a nightmare. You may want to consider a policy of accepting no late papers, allowing a student to work on the late assignment within twenty-four hours of the due date to receive a fixed amount of extra credit, or using the voucher system. (See pages 172–174 for more information on vouchers.) Consider recording no grades until papers requiring a parental signature are returned.

4. What is your policy regarding papers with no names?

Consider the message you want to send to your students about responsibility. Depending on the age of the students, they should be able to consistently put their names on their papers. (Kindergarten through first grade would be a reasonable exception.) Do you have the time and should you make the time to hunt for students to sign their papers? Consider requiring that students' names be on their papers in order to receive credit for their work. Be sure to post this rule of "no name, no credit" in full view of all students and discuss it with them at the beginning of the course. Include this in your short list of classroom rules to be signed by parents and students. There might be a few heartbreaking experiences early in the year, but students are quick to learn.

5. What amount of student involvement in lesson planning, grading papers in class, assembling bulletin boards, policy making, setting grading guidelines, and teacher evaluations do you expect?

Lesson Planning—While you should make the basic decisions about the curriculum (information students need to learn, the order of skills, etc.), whenever possible and appropriate—and under your guidance and with your approval—let students help decide how to utilize the materials, which materials to use, etc. Remember, within reason, the more student input, the more student output.

Grading Papers in Class—Check with state, district, and building policies. With the exception of tests and subjective essays, grading papers in class helps students learn more because it allows them another review of the material. Students are also able to receive prompt feedback. On occasion, review a set of papers to ensure that they are being corrected accurately by the students. Having students sign the papers they correct helps make them more responsible.

Assembling Bulletin Boards—Having students help with the design and assembly of bulletin boards is a great way to instill their pride in the classroom.

Policy Making—Listen closely and openly to student suggestions regarding classroom policy and include any of their suggestions that are reasonable; however, do not let students talk you out of or into any rules about which you feel strongly.

Setting Grading Guidelines—When appropriate, allow students to have input regarding the amount of points possible on some assignments or projects. Keep in mind that allowing student input to affect the grading scale or the method used to total the points for quarter or semester grades is inappropriate. At times, though, you may want to negotiate on due dates for large projects or on some test dates. You may not realize that many of your students' other teachers have chosen that same date for tests of their own. Short class discussions can reveal a great deal of valuable information, and students will respect the fact that you ask for their input. An honest and sincere effort on your part to listen to students tells them you respect their opinions. If you do this as often as is possible, students will be much more likely to respect your decisions. Keep these discussions short, and don't allow sidetracking.

Teacher Evaluations—Who is better equipped to evaluate you than the people with whom you spend the most time? While the thought of being evaluated by your students may be intimidating, the outcome will most likely be positive as student feedback helps you know in which direction to steer classroom instruction. Most students are honest in their criticism and generous with positive reinforcement. Be sure to construct the evaluation in a positive manner.

6. Will you allow gum, food, beverages, hats, etc., in the classroom?

Decide if you are supervising a fast-food restaurant, a playground, or a classroom. You can do a good job at only one of these tasks. Remember that there are enough distractions in the classroom without intentionally allowing additional ones. The more distractions you can eliminate, the more learning will take place in your classroom. There are plenty of times and places for kids to enjoy food and beverages and to wear hats: the classroom should not be one of them.

7. What is your policy regarding persistent tardies?

Students are responsible for persistent tardies, not you. Do not be fooled by a student's excuses regarding persistent tardies or let that student's behavior disrupt your teaching, add stress, or make you angry. You deserve more respect, and so do the students who arrive on time. To stop this problem, try giving short and easy quizzes as soon as class begins, and allow only those students with excused absences to make them up. Students will understand your message very quickly.

8. Do you intend to make available your home phone number and encourage students to call you?

Making your phone number available to your students encourages both students and parents to call you at home. If you want your privacy, do not give out your home phone number. Unless you are unlisted, your students will be able to locate you in an emergency.

9. Do you intend to stay after school on a regular basis to tutor students?

If a student expresses a sincere desire to learn, then offer to stay. However, be aware of overdoing a good thing; you may begin to suffer "burn out." Always make yourself available to help students during fixed office hours, but be realistic in your expectations of yourself.

10. What is your policy regarding office hours?

Decide on your office hours, discuss them with your students, and then post them on your classroom door. Try not to make exceptions for a particular student or change your office hours unless absolutely necessary. You may, however, want to be considerate of parental requests to meet at other times due to their work schedules. At the same time, remember to be fair to yourself and reasonable about the amount of time you spend at school.

11. What is your policy regarding students leaving during class and what are acceptable reasons for doing so?

Consider this policy: "No one leaves the room during class except for an emergency or signed hall pass." Take note of students who make a habit of inventing emergencies or who frequently have signed notes from the counseling department, the office, etc., during your class, and become familiar with authentic administrative signatures. Word travels quickly if you uphold your policy, and, for the most part, very few students will leave your room. A positive reply to a rather dubious excuse is: "Nice try." Remember to say it with a smile!

12. What is your policy regarding students leaving class once it has begun to retrieve homework or papers from their lockers?

Even the most conscientious students can forget to bring materials and assignments to class, and while it is hard to tell them that they cannot leave the room, what is fair for one is fair for all. If you allow students to leave your class in order to retrieve assignments, you may find that a good many students will be at their lockers when your class begins. Consider how much teaching time you are willing to sacrifice to students' lack of organization. To maintain order in your classroom, enforce a policy that requires all students to come prepared to class. Students who forget their work once or twice may use the voucher system (see pages 172–174).

13. What is your policy regarding students leaving class during tests?

During test time, reinforce the policy that no one leaves the classroom unless in an emergency.

14. What is your policy regarding students who do not complete tests and want more time later in the day?

If a learning disabled (or otherwise impaired) student needs additional time to take an exam, make arrangements with a resource teacher or other appropriate staff member to have the student complete the test under his or her supervision, or allow that student to stay in your classroom during the next period to complete the test, if possible. If you know ahead of time that a student will need extra time taking a test, the best idea is to arrange a plan with the resource teacher or the teacher who has the student in class after your period. Another alternative is to give the learning disabled student an oral test on the same day as the regular test.

When considering whether other students may have additional time to complete an exam, remember that allowing a student to begin the test in the classroom, leave the classroom, and then return to complete the test no longer provides an accurate assessment for that individual. In other words, what started as a test ends up as an in-class assignment completed over two time periods. Ask yourself what your objective is in giving the test before coming to a decision on this issue. Of course, you should construct tests so that they can be completed during one class period.

15. When are papers due in class (at the beginning of class or by the end of class)?

Make it a habit to include this bit of information when giving any assignment. For example, you might say: "This assignment will be due first thing when class begins tomorrow" or "This assignment will be due at the end of the period tomorrow, and you may have the entire class period to work on it." It is important that you collect the assignments when you say you will. If you do not, you may lose your students' trust: those students who work hard to complete their assignments on time will think it unfair and may begin to come to class unprepared.

16. When will you remove students from the classroom because of negative behavior?

Become familiar with your school's policy regarding when, how, and where to remove very disruptive students from the classroom. Some faculties follow a formal procedure; others do not and allow the individual teacher to set his or her own policy. If this is the case, consider the following strategies. (Keep in mind that you should leave your classroom only in an emergency situation.) It is a good idea to state in writing your policy regarding disruptive students and removal from the classroom, as well as inform any administrators or counselors. You should also attempt to handle all discipline problems yourself. Students will respect you more for it. Only in extreme situations should you turn a discipline case over to someone else.

A great deal of negative behavior can be disarmed by keeping calm, maintaining control of yourself and the classroom, and implementing a warning system which students understand (see pages 124–129). If a student's behavior escalates beyond the warning stage, it is a good idea to remove him or her from the class-room and thus away from an audience. By doing this, you shift the balance of power away from the student and into your own hands. In many cases, when removed from the curious eyes of fellow classmates, a disruptive student will lose his or her bravado. Once the student is isolated, insist on his or her undivided attention and maintain control by asking the student specific and direct questions concerning his or her behavior. *Carefully word your questions and comments so that it is clear to the student that you are attacking his or her behavior, not person.* You might first ask: "What were you doing in class to disrupt the learning atmosphere?" or "What behavior were you using that caused you to be removed from the classroom?" After the student has admitted to his or her disruptive behavior, you might ask: "Why were you acting that way?" "What do you need to do (or change) before you're allowed back into the class?" "If you choose not to change your behavior, do you know what the next step will be?" Listen to the student's replies, and do not let him or her back into the classroom until you are satisfied with what you hear. If the student refuses to cooperate with you, your final step should be to escort that student to the office of the administrator in charge of student discipline, briefly review your actions and the student's responses, and tell the administrator that you will contact him or her at your earliest opportunity. If you cannot leave the classroom in order to escort a disruptive student to the office, you may want to use the intercom, pager, or phone system to call for an administrator or send a trusted student to fetch the administrator in charge.

17. Will you allow students to look at their grades in your gradebook?

If you have established a system that allows students to keep track of their own grades (for more information on this subject, see pages 159–165) and you continually update their list of assignments (see pages 132–140), there will be no need for students to view your gradebook. Some students are very sensitive about their grades and prefer to keep them private. Their decision should be respected. You may want to use student ID numbers to post test, midterm, or final grades.

18. What is your policy regarding student use of unacceptable language in the classroom?

From the first day of class, let students know how you feel about inappropriate language. Most students use unacceptable and inappropriate language for its shock value. If you don't pay much attention to this behavior, it will probably dissipate (at least around you). Tell your class that you respect students and that you expect the same respect from them. Using racial, religious, or sexual slurs of any type, profanity, or abusive language shows a lack of respect to anyone within earshot and demonstrates a lack of self-respect from the person who uses such language. It is wise, however, not to place too much emphasis on your methods of enforcing this policy. Simply demonstrate that there is no time to bother with such behavior and that it is a waste of the student's time to continue with it. Firmly deal with it the first time a student uses poor language, and then go on.

19. May students take back papers after they have been turned in?

Once a paper has been turned in, it should remain turned in. The only exceptions might be the immediate (within one minute) addition of a forgotten name, date, assignment number, etc. Simple additions such as these are acceptable, but do not allow a student to change or add any answers. If a particular student seems to make a habit of this type of behavior, speak to that student, privately telling him or her that he or she is taking unfair advantage of the rule and needs to stop.

20. Where do you expect students to be when class begins?

Your organization can prevent the majority of discipline problems from ever surfacing. Remember that the "action" message you give speaks louder than the "word." From the beginning of the year, demonstrate that you are ready to begin class on time and expect that students will be as well. You may choose to begin each class with a sponge activity (see pages 281–283), a short quiz, a creative attention grabber (see pages 284–285), or other activity for which students need to be in their seats and ready to work. If you implement this type of system, your students will soon learn that they do not have time to waste in your classroom. It is important to keep in mind that it takes about two weeks to make a habit and about six weeks to break one. If you reveal your expectations to your students from the beginning of class, it should take two weeks or less for all students to be in their seats and ready to begin class on time. On the other hand, if you allow students to break your rules during the first few weeks of class, you can plan on about six weeks of retraining time.

21. How do you expect students to behave when you are called out of the room?

If it is necessary to leave the classroom, remind students that they are expected to behave as if you were present. Before stepping into your room when you return, it is a good idea to pause for a few seconds to quietly observe the students. If there are any significant disruptions, all students involved should be handed some form of punishment, such as writing a discipline letter (see "Sign Up: A Discipline System That Works," pages 124–129) or remaining at school for detention.

22. What is your policy regarding students losing handouts and wanting you to copy additional ones for them?

Make two or three extra copies of handouts and place them on your potpourri table (see page 146). When these copies are gone, do not replace them. Students need to be responsible for organizing their own papers. Once you are sure that every student has received a copy of the handout, your responsibility ends. Should a student lose his or her copy and none are found in the box on the potpourri table, it should be the student's responsibility to find or make another copy—otherwise, you will find yourself wasting valuable time making numerous and needless trips to the production room. This is one important method of demonstrating responsibility to your students and helping them become independent learners.

23. How do you respond to negative student behavior directed toward a substitute teacher?

Explain your policy regarding substitute teachers at the beginning of the year. Discuss with your students how they might feel if they had the responsibilities of a substitute teacher. Ask them what type of behavior they would appreciate and not appreciate if in such a position and if they view substitute teachers as people who are trying to do their best in strange surroundings. Inform your students that you will support the teacher who takes your place and follow through with any recommendations, decisions, and comments he or she might make. Never undermine a substitute's authority by speaking negatively about him or her in front of students. If your substitute teacher does not carry out your plans or proves to be unsatisfactory, call the substitute office and inform them not to assign that particular teacher to your class again. If the situation warrants further action, discuss it with your principal or the administrator in charge.

24. What is your policy regarding making up tests?

Deciding whether or not to issue a make-up exam depends on the exam, the situation, and the student. If you choose to do so, consider giving a more difficult oral exam to a student you suspect of skipping your class because of the original test. These types of tests are quick to assess and grade and do not require much additional time on your part. However, sometimes it is better to give a written test. Remember that students who have missed a test have an advantage over those who took the test in class. Be realistic. Know that questions and answers are shared after tests. Use your good judgement to decide on an appropriate and fair make-up test. You can give the student the same exam, develop a new one, assign an alternative paper or activity, or give an oral test.

25. What is your policy regarding paraprofessional aids, student assistants, or parent volunteers entering grades in the gradebook or on a computer?

This decision is a personal one. Grades, or any type of evaluative instrument, are important, and keeping errors to a minimum when recording them is imperative. While you may save yourself some time assigning this task to someone else, in order to maintain confidentiality and overall responsibility for grading, you may want to complete this task yourself. There are other tasks you can assign to aids and volunteers.

26. What is your policy regarding students who come to class unprepared (with no paper, pen or pencil, book, etc.)?

Everyone occasionally forgets to bring supplies to class. Ask the student who occasionally forgets his or her supplies to borrow materials or share a book with another student. However, for the student who seems to make a habit of coming to class unprepared, there are other solutions. Depending upon the age of the student, try some of these ideas: letting the student keep a pencil or pen in one of your desk drawers, letting the student donate looseleaf notebook paper to the potpourri table, letting the student do without for the class period, subtracting a given amount of extra credit points, establishing a point system for being prepared and including it as a portion of the grade for that class, or having the student write a note to him- or herself each day materials are forgotten.

"HALF OF 8 IS 3"

"No."

"Not quite."

"Please try again."

"O.K. How did you come up with that?"

"Very interesting. Can you explain your answer?"

*"I'm sorry, that's not quite the answer
I was looking for."*

*"Good try, Johnny. Can anyone
help him with a better answer?"*

"Great! What are other possible answers?"

Which one of these statements would have been your response to the student who creatively (and correctly) answered "Half of 8 is 3"? This student's response proves that sometimes even the most straightforward questions have more than one answer. There is more than one way to approach and solve many of the tasks we accomplish every day, and there is no best way to teach anything—only what works well for a good teacher. When listening to a student's response, it is often more important to understand his or her thinking process (the way he or she arrived at an answer using left or right brain thinking) than to receive the expected answer. Asking a student to analyze his or her thinking process produces a number of positive results for the student, the class as a whole, and for you! The student will understand more clearly the subject matter being discussed. Listening to another student's correct or incorrect response will reinforce the rest of the class's grasp of the material or point out flaws in their own thinking. Understanding your students' thinking processes will help you become a better teacher as you will be able to glean important ideas about your students' creative thinking processes and incorporate them the next time you teach this concept. You will also be able to point out some incorrect ways of approaching the concept as well as some common problems students encounter the first time they learn the concept. Your students will think you are a genius!

Another important reason to analyze students' thinking is to ascertain their particular learning styles. Each of us has a unique learning style that requires us to use different techniques to absorb and process information. A good teacher should be aware of these differences in his or her students and help students become aware of them in themselves. The information in the following section will help you appreciate the different learning styles students demonstrate and adapt your teaching approaches to better meet your students' needs.

LEARNING STYLES

Though the human brain functions as a whole, it is actually divided into two hemispheres (the left and the right) which act, react, think, process, and solve problems in very different ways. In each person, one side of the brain is usually dominant. The list on the following page provides a brief profile of typical left and right brain dominance characteristics. In addition to being left- or right-brain dominant, each person learns through one of three basic modalities: visual (seeing), auditory (hearing), and kinesthetic (feeling, doing). For characteristics specific to these different learning modalities, refer to page 37. Understanding these profiles and how each of your students fits within them can make a big difference in the effectiveness of your teaching. You may want to refer to page 38, "Suggested Aids for Learning Modalities," to help a student find a different way to process information. You can share the following three pages with students in the form of handouts or project them on the overhead during a discussion.

To accommodate all students, it is a good idea to teach using a variety of approaches and activities. Suggestions for varying the presentation of a lesson to accommodate different learning styles are included in "Using Learning Styles in the Classroom" on page 39. Further suggestions for help with a particular student who is having difficulty learning are included in "Learning Style Applications for an Individual Student" on page 40. Individual brain dominance and modality assessments can be found in *Learning to Learn, Revised Edition,* pages 17–19, and 23–25, Incentive Publications, 2004.

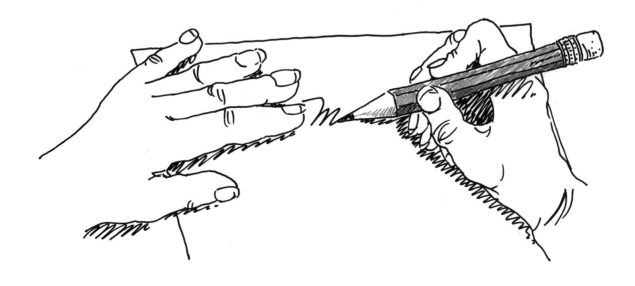

LEFT/RIGHT BRAIN DOMINANCE CHARACTERISTICS

LEFT

- sequential
- intellectual
- structured/planned
- controls feelings
- analytical
- logical
- remembers names
- rational
- solves problems by breaking them apart
- time oriented
- auditory/visual learner
- prefers to write and talk
- follows spoken directions
- talks to think and learn
- prefers T/F, multiple-choice and matching tests
- takes few risks (with control)
- looks for the differences
- controls right side of body
- thinks mathematically
- thinks concretely
- language abilities
- thinks of one thing at a time

RIGHT

- holistic
- intuitive
- spontaneous
- lets feelings go
- creative/responsive
- more abstract
- remembers faces
- more likely to act on emotions
- solves problems by looking at the whole
- spatially oriented
- kinesthetic learner
- prefers to draw and handle objects
- follows written or demonstrated directions
- "pictures" things to think and learn
- prefers essay tests
- takes more risks (less control)
- looks for similar qualities
- controls left side of body
- musical abilities
- emotional
- thinks simultaneously

From *Learning To Learn, Rev. Ed.* by Gloria Frender.
Nashville, TN: Incentive Publications, ©2004. Used by permission.

Teaching for Learning Success, Rev. Ed.

CHARACTERISTICS OF LEARNING STYLES

Three of your five senses are used primarily in learning, storing, remembering, and recalling information. Your eyes, ears, and sense of touch play essential roles in the way you communicate, perceive reality, and relate to others. Because you learn from and communicate best with someone who shares your dominant modality, it is a great advantage for you to know the characteristics of visual, auditory, and kinesthetic learning styles and to be able to identify them in others.

VISUAL	AUDITORY	KINESTHETIC
• mind sometimes strays during verbal activities	• talks to self aloud	• likes physical rewards
• observes rather than talks or acts	• enjoys talking	• in motion most of the time
• organized in approach to tasks	• easily distracted	• likes to touch people when talking to them
• likes to read	• has more difficulty with written directions	• taps pencil or foot while studying
• usually a good speller	• likes to be read to	• enjoys doing activities
• memorizes by seeing graphics and pictures	• memorizes by steps in a sequence	• reading is not a priority
• not too distractible	• enjoys music	• poor speller
• finds verbal instructions difficult	• whispers to self while reading	• likes to solve problems by physically working through them
• has good handwriting	• remembers faces	• will try new things
• remembers faces	• easily distracted by noises	• outgoing by nature; expresses emotions through physical means
• uses advanced planning	• hums or sings	• uses hands while talking
• doodles	• outgoing by nature	• dresses for comfort
• quiet by nature	• enjoys listening activities	• enjoys handling objects
• meticulous, neat in appearance		
• notices details		

Students who have equal modality preferences are more flexible learners and are already using many studying techniques rather than just a few.

From *Learning To Learn, Rev. Ed.* by Gloria Frender. Nashville, TN: Incentive Publications, ©2004. Used by permission.

Depending on which learning modality you determined was dominant for you, use these aids to sharpen your particular dominant learning modality or to strengthen a weaker one. Try to be aware of the different activities you do daily to develop all three modalities.

VISUAL

- use guided imagery
- form pictures in your mind
- take notes
- see parts of words
- use "cue" words
- use notebooks
- use color coding
- use study/flash cards
- use photographic pictures
- watch filmstrips
- watch movies
- use charts, graphs
- use maps
- demonstrate
- create and use drawings
- use exhibits
- watch lips move in front of a mirror
- use mnemonics (mind maps, visual chains, acronyms, acrostics, hook-ups)

AUDITORY

- use tapes
- watch TV
- listen to music
- speak and listen to speakers
- make up rhymes or poems
- read aloud
- talk to yourself
- repeat things orally
- use rhythmic sounds
- have discussions
- listen carefully
- use oral directions
- sound out words
- use theater
- say words in syllables
- use mnemonics (word links, rhymes, poems, lyrics)

KINESTHETIC

- pace or walk as you study
- physically "do it"
- practice by repeated motion
- breathe slowly
- role play
- exercise
- dance
- write
- write on surfaces with finger
- take notes
- associate feelings with concept/information
- write lists repeatedly
- stretch and move in chair
- watch lips move in front of a mirror
- use mnemonics (word links, rhymes, poems, lyrics)

From *Learning To Learn, Rev. Ed.* by Gloria Frender. Nashville, TN: Incentive Publications, ©2004. Used by permission.

Teaching for Learning Success, Rev. Ed.

USING LEARNING STYLES
IN THE CLASSROOM

◆ **Know students' learning styles.**

◆ **Teach students to recognize their individual learning styles.**

◆ **Vary learning activities. Include these attributes in all your lesson plans:**

Vary group size:

- independent
- paired
- small group
- large group

Vary surroundings:

- noise level
- quiet
- seating arrangement

Vary teaching approaches and materials:

- left/right brain
- auditory
- visual
- kinesthetic

Vary your presentation style:

- minilecture
- lecture
- student presentation
- hands-on discovery
- questioning
- games

◆ **Identify and match materials to modalities; offer students suggestions on ways to adapt other learning styles.**

◆ **State objective and expected outcome.**

◆ **Guide students through each activity; elicit a few responses when appropriate.**

LEARNING STYLE APPLICATIONS FOR AN INDIVIDUAL STUDENT

Step 1   Think of a student in your class who is having problems understanding basic concepts.

Step 2   Based on the information you know about learning styles, which learning style characteristics does this student display? Talk to the student for his or her input.

Step 3   What types of activities do you usually use in your classroom? Are any of them directed toward this student's learning style?

Step 4   What other types of activities or teaching strategies could you incorporate into your lessons which might better accommodate this student's learning style?

Step 5   Try one or two of these new strategies.

Step 6   What changes, if any, have happened as a result of your choices?

Step 7   What should you do next? Repeat the strategy? Try another one?

Step 8   Make a note to follow through on your conclusions.

Teaching for Learning Success, Rev. Ed.

ACTIVE VS. PASSIVE LEARNING

True learning occurs when information is received, processed, and stored using active learning strategies that best suit an individual's learning style.

(Author's Note: Be sure to share the following important information with students.)

For most of us, by the second time we read information written on a page, our mind has absorbed all that it is going to understand from that material. Therefore, the third, fourth, and fifth reading of the same handouts or class notes in the same way is a waste of time. To truly understand, transfer, apply, memorize, or recall that information, you need to become an active participant in the learning process and do something with the information—not just let it remain on the paper.

When you apply all of your senses to learning and actively manipulate the information, true learning is the result. Impress upon your students that learning can be made exciting and take much less time than most of them already spend studying. **Studying smart involves using strategies that work with your brain instead of against it.**

Review with students the information on the following page, "Using All Your Senses to Learn." Share the learning checklist on page 43 with students by making a transparency of it for use during a class discussion, copying and distributing it as a handout for students to include in their binders, or enlarging it for use as a poster in your classroom. Using it all three ways is best. Specific learning strategies are also mentioned on the following pages: "Super Study Sheets" (pages 232–234), "Graphic Organizers" (pages 235–247), and "Memory Tips" (pages 262–273).

USING ALL YOUR SENSES TO LEARN

By using all of your senses when studying, information is retained longer, and you make more efficient and effective use of your study time. The handout on the following page outlines a simple process for incorporating all of the senses when studying. Discuss with students the steps involved in this process (see information below). Enlarge the handout on page 43 to make a poster for your room, use it as a transparency to be displayed during a class discussion, or make each student a handout to include in his or her binder or notebook as a reminder of good study skills.

HEAR IT: Encourage students to talk to themselves (if appropriate) when studying. If they say the information, they will also hear it. One exception might be when reading prose, as it slows down reading rate.

SEE IT: Look at the information at the same time it is said and heard.

SAY IT: Repeat aloud the information several times.

WRITE IT: Become an active learner by manipulating the information through taking notes and using index cards. Don't let it just remain on the page.

DO IT: Use motion; walk or pace as you talk, and act out the information. Occasionally, get up from your desk or chair to review flash cards, notes, etc.

These steps turn passive learners into active learners. Every learning style modality is used, helping students retain focused learning longer. **Students learn more when they can interact with information rather than simply react to it.**

Teaching for Learning Success, Rev. Ed.

REMEMBER . . .

Use all of your senses
when you learn:

 **Hear It**

See It

Say It

Write It

— **Do It** *!* —

TEACHING THROUGH
THE BACK DOOR

"Teaching through the back door? Isn't it easier to use the front door?"
Yes, sometimes, but it isn't as interesting, effective, or memorable.

The front door approach to teaching is a formal, structured lecture approach that has been used in the classroom for years. This approach often begins with the teacher stating the topic for the day followed by a minilecture or lecture through which information is shared. The teacher presents the information, and students are expected to take notes and work on handouts individually or in groups. The end of class is typically set aside for student questions and a brief summary of the main concepts. The essentials are all included in this method of teaching: introduction of the topic, sharing of information, and a conclusion. Often, however, this approach neglects to capture students' attention, create excitement for the subject, tap the curiosity of the participants, demonstrate the reasons the material is important to know, model how to learn, and make the most of a learning atmosphere. In short, it is passive learning. Use it sparingly.

The back door approach to teaching is one without a formula or system. It is a philosophy based on the notion that in order for real learning to take place, students must utilize thinking, focusing, and questioning techniques which allow them to discover concepts for themselves and successfully apply them to real-life situations. It is active learning. Research shows that people learn more and retain information longer when they are completely engaged in the learning process. Concepts are transferred and applied more effectively through intentional practice, and information is absorbed more quickly when students take part in discovering information for themselves. In other words, learning is increased when students actively participate in the learning process rather than function as passive observers. Enthusiasm and excitement are highly contagious! If you begin the school year by "teaching through the back door," you will find that your students will be more receptive to and excited about the information you are teaching.

So, how do you teach "through the back door"? Tap your creativity and think of new ways to approach your subject that will excite and engage students. (Remember that a good teacher is about one-quarter entertainer. Be physically active and move around the classroom.) Guide students to discover ideas and concepts for themselves. Engage them in their own learning and actively model higher-level thinking skills and problem-solving techniques by providing exciting "hooks" at the beginning of the class and channeling constructive questions for active participation. Allow time at the end of class for a summary of the information, and provide opportunities for the immediate application of information through challenging and meaningful assignments.

A list of suggestions to make teaching more exciting follows. Not all of the ideas will be of use to you; apply and adapt the ones which best fit with your own teaching style.

Teaching for Learning Success, Rev. Ed.

1. Use a variety of activities to "hook" students at the beginning of class.

- Introduce a sponge activity (see pages 281–283).

- Make use of creative attention grabbers (see pages 284–285).

- Ask leading questions instead of giving answers.

- Vary your "hook" strategies. Students enjoy wondering what the opening activity will be when they walk into class.

- Be dynamic and energetic (even on those days you do not feel like it).

2. When introducing a new concept, use leading questions to allow students to discover the lesson's main ideas, find out why the information is important, and how to best learn it. Always combine why and how with what.

- Ask questions that focus students' thinking on the concept.

- Ask questions that help students uncover the lesson's main ideas.

- Ask students to discuss what they already know about the concept or subject, linking old information with the new.

- Ask students to think of how they might use this information in the future. You also might want to share with them some experiences of your own related to this subject.

- Discuss why this information is important to students.

- Give students the whole picture. (This method will especially capture the interest and understanding of the right-brain learner.)

- Break down the concept into smaller parts and show the relationship among those parts. (This method will especially capture the interest and understanding of the left-brain learner.)

- Involve students in active participation. Lead students to discover the necessary information through guided questions rather than simply telling them the facts.

- Use visual aids, such as the chalkboard or dry-erase board, overhead transparencies, pictures, posters, models, etc., at every opportunity. Use auditory media whenever practical and appropriate. Provide a one or two minute class break or do some physical activity to help those kinesthetic learners.

3. Apply the concept.

- Encourage students to apply the information within various group arrangements (individual, pair, small or large group).

- Use a variety of student-created materials that are directed toward each learning modality (visual, auditory, kinesthetic). They are very successful.

- Make use of graphic organizers (see pages 235–247) for guided listening and note taking or review.

- Introduce to the class any activity which makes students organize and manipulate the information into a different format. Encourage those left-brain functions.

- Encourage oral interaction among students, but be aware that students may need to be directed back to the subject at times.

- Design new and interesting assignments which will tap your students' imaginations. Encourage those right-brain functions!

- Depending on the age level and maturity of your students, include them as much as possible in the planning of activities and assignments. You may find yourself pleasantly surprised by their innovations, and they will be much more responsive to you if you listen to their suggestions.

- Assign work that is meaningful, adds to the students' understanding of the concept, and provides practice for review.

- Provide assignments that encourage upper-level thinking attributes (analysis, synthesis, evaluation).

4. Allow summary and question time.

- Use class summary logs (see pages 218–221).

- Ask a variety of students to orally summarize main concepts.

- Review directions and expectations for each assignment.

- Allow time for students to write down assignments.

5. Action Checklist

Did you remember to:

___ physically model active learning (move around the room, change voice inflection and pitch, demonstrate excitement for the subject being discussed)?

___ demonstrate why the material is important?

___ use a variety of "hooks" to interest students?

___ ask leading questions and encourage higher-level thinking skills?

___ present the information as a whole or break it down into its integral parts?

___ use aids that are directed toward a variety of learning styles and modalities (visual, auditory, kinesthetic, left/right brain)?

___ teach students how to learn along with what to learn?

___ assign immediate, meaningful tasks that apply the information?

___ allow time for a summary activity?

Always combine

WHY

and

HOW

with

WHAT

you study.

GIVING STUDENTS FEEDBACK

Feedback is one of the most important communication skills that can be developed between student and teacher. All students need feedback in order to learn. Positive feedback allows students to focus their thinking, better understand their individual learning processes, and clarify or change content ideas. Make providing feedback a priority in your classroom.

VERBAL FEEDBACK

- Hold class discussions instead of lectures when possible. Employ guided questioning techniques that involve students and help them to uncover concepts on their own. Encourage active learning through active participation. (See pages 44–46, "Teaching Through the Back Door.")

- Take the time to respond to individual students. For every student that asks a question, one-third of the students in the classroom have the same question.

- Before returning graded assignments, give a brief overview of the positive aspects of the assignment as well as areas that need improvement. This gives students a better idea of what you were thinking and looking for when grading their papers.

- Use seatwork as a diagnostic instrument. Make it a point to give students ample time when working on an in-class assignment and to circulate among students while they work. Briefly respond to each individual, and let each student know if he or she is using the correct thinking process, if he or she is "on track" or missing the point, etc. By correcting thinking and production errors early, students will have a much better chance of successfully completing the assignment.

- Learn to use positive and constructive words instead of negative ones. You can point out weaknesses and express negative ideas in a positive way. Be careful not to give oral responses that immediately discourage students from further involvement in the lesson. "That's an interesting question. What's your thinking behind it?"

- Create excitement about the subject by encouraging students to respond to other students through class discussion instead of only addressing you with their feedback.

WRITTEN FEEDBACK

- Grade, record, and return all student work within 2–3 days. Research shows that the more time that elapses between completion of a task and receiving feedback on that task, the less meaningful the feedback becomes.

Teaching for Learning Success, Rev. Ed.

- Never write only the points or grade at the top of the paper. Students will remember teacher comments longer than any score or grade. Written feedback gives specific direction for improvement; scores and grades do not. Depending on the type, length, and complexity of the assignment, always write a response that is appropriate to the work completed. For example, a five-minute quiz given at the beginning of class would rate the score or grade and a one- or two-word comment: "Great," "Nice Try," "Improving," etc. A research paper, full lab report, comprehensive critique, or a book review deserves detailed commentary. Because most students value the time they spent completing an assignment, they appreciate the time you take to write thoughtful, helpful comments. Make a point to include the grade within your comments so students must read what you wrote rather than simply looking at the grade at the top and ignoring your helpful commentary.

- Personal interaction with every student every day is often difficult for a number of reasons. Lack of time, size and structure of classes, and quiet, shy students who do not actively participate in class discussions are all too often the cause of infrequent student/teacher communication. For a few students, written commentary may be the only opportunity to receive direct feedback.

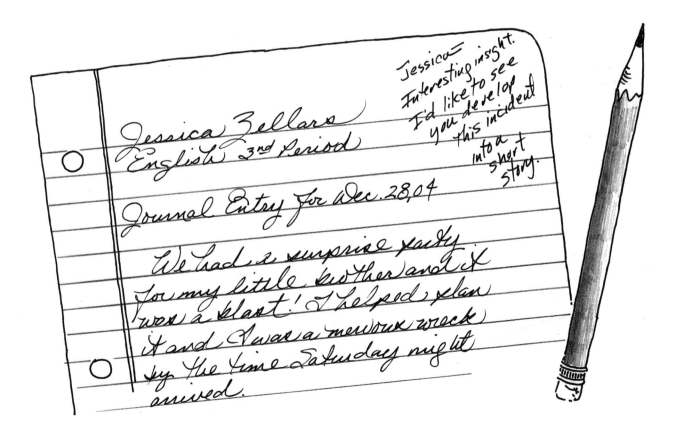

LESSON PLANNING

Writing a lesson plan is a little like buying a car: you analyze your needs and look for a product that satisfies them. While there are plenty of models from which to choose, you will purchase only what you need (and can afford). As with cars, there is a variety of lesson plans available. Your choice will depend upon your needs, including:

- curriculum guidelines
- your sense of direction
- your plan of organization
- variety to meet students' needs
- the amount of time available

Let's briefly examine each of these basic criteria.

Curriculum Guidelines

Most school districts make use of curriculum guides which outline the contents to be taught in each class or grade level. All lesson plans must incorporate these guidelines. When planning, make an organized list of units and concepts that must be covered in the course. (Refer to the example on pages 57–59, "Brief Curriculum Guide Across Three Grade Levels.") Make a new copy of the lists each year and cross off the units and concepts as you teach them. You may find that in teaching one unit you include many concepts from all of the major categories. However, do not be surprised if you do not manage to teach all of the concepts by the end of the year. It is far better to teach a little less of a subject with greater student comprehension than more with greater student confusion.

Sense of Direction

Now that you have developed a useable guide of concepts to cover, map out a general timeline. (Use the "Unit Planning Calendar" forms on pages 61–62.) Be sure to write your timeline in pencil, as it is sure to change. No matter how much it changes, however, this is worth doing because it helps keep your teaching plans focused throughout the school year.

Plan of Organization

Whether you work better from detailed plans or a simple list, remember to keep your plans organized. Read through the unit plan suggestions on pages 52–56.

Variety to Meet Students' Needs

Good teachers teach to all learning styles, vary the types of activities, and find interesting and enthusiastic ways of engaging students. You may want to write down your techniques, either by making a step-by-step list or jotting down a few words and listing the necessary materials.

Amount of Time Available

Never take more time to create a lesson plan than to teach it. Lesson plans are meant to serve as a basic structure for your teaching. They should never overpower or take away from your enthusiasm and teaching style. If creating lesson plans becomes more of a hindrance than a help, it is time to try another format.

The following pages present suggestions and ideas for creating a variety of lesson plans, from the formal and detailed outline to the quick checklist. You may find just what you are looking for, or you may want to modify, combine, or create a completely new plan using only some of the ideas. And remember, like a newly purchased car, a lesson plan can always use a little fine tuning and an occasional polish.

UNIT PLAN SUGGESTIONS:
An Introduction

Lesson plans can be useful tools with which to organize strategies and materials for optimal teaching and learning. A good lesson plan makes teaching easier, more enjoyable, and less stressful. It should be thorough, yet easy to follow; it is intended to keep you from "reinventing the wheel" each time you reteach a unit or a concept. At the same time, a good lesson plan should be flexible enough to allow you to adjust to changing student needs. Label and file these plans for future references.

Developing a unit plan involves organizing a subject by unit and then analyzing each unit to identify the basic concepts you wish to cover. Knowing ahead of time the concepts you want to cover in each unit saves both time and energy when planning a specific lesson. Because unit plans are basic (you are working with only the framework of a lesson), they are flexible. While you may keep a unit plan for many years, it will continually change as you add to it new ideas and materials to meet student needs. (Using three-ring binders allows for the easy addition and removal of materials as well as keeps papers and materials more secure. They are also easier to transport than file folders. Use various colored tabs to break down sections of the units.) In addition to basic concepts, establish and record a wide variety of ancillary materials appropriate to teaching each unit. (Refer to pages 78–81, "Materials at Your Fingertips: Creating a Cross-reference of Enrichment Materials," for additional suggestions.)

The unit plan system has been proven highly successful. Read through the following pages of suggestions once to ascertain the main ideas and details of the system. Then reread the material to note any changes you might want to make in order to adapt the plans to your particular teaching needs and style. The unit plan can be used with any of the lesson plans which follow.

UNIT PLAN SUGGESTIONS:
Where Lesson Plans Begin

WHAT

Unit plans encompass one major aspect of the curriculum and contain specific lesson plans that teach concepts and details within that unit. For example, Geology is a unit of Earth Science. A specific lesson plan in Geology might cover the concept of land forms or rock formations.

WHY

A unit plan:

- ◆ keeps you organized and on track
- ◆ provides an overview of the entire unit and shows how major topics and specific concepts fit together within that unit
- ◆ saves time and energy
- ◆ is efficient—all materials are organized and in one place
- ◆ allows you the time to plan for a greater variety of teaching strategies
- ◆ provides the opportunity to gather a greater selection of enrichment materials and helps prevent comments such as: "I wish I had known about this material last month!"
- ◆ lends itself to excellent substitute plans that are easy to compile
- ◆ allows you to work on lesson plans in advance—once you have one unit thoroughly planned for several weeks, you can begin work on future units
- ◆ provides for more flexibility as you are ready to move ahead or skip around in your plan if necessary
- ◆ can easily be divided into daily plans that better suit your students' pace

MATERIALS

- ◆ three-ring binder (allows more flexibility than a notebook when adding or deleting materials)
- ◆ loose-leaf notebook paper
- ◆ multiple copies of the blank form for specific lesson plans (see pages 65, 67, 69)
- ◆ additional paper binder pockets (a place to keep transparencies or pages that cannot be three-hole punched, additional materials for bulletin board displays, etc.)
- ◆ colored plastic tab dividers or tabbed divider pages for each main concept within the unit
- ◆ district or school curriculum guides
- ◆ file cabinets or shelves

UNIT PLAN SUGGESTIONS

HOW

1. First, become familiar with district and/or school curriculum guides or any other guides that might affect the curriculum. Locate and read the criteria relating to each subject and content area. Break it down into manageable, appropriate units. Keep copies with the unit plans.

2. List the major curriculum categories. For example, some of the major curriculum categories from the sample curriculum on pages 57–59 are: vocabulary development, grammar/sentence skills, mechanics, and reference skills.

3. Summarize the curriculum by listing single concepts within these major categories. For example, some of the concepts listed in the vocabulary development category on page 57 are prefixes, suffixes, and roots. This list will serve as a checklist once the entire unit is assembled.

4. Whenever possible, make a list of the concepts being taught in these categories in both one grade level above and below the one you are currently teaching. This provides a good sense of continuum, helps you become more informed when answering parent questions, and saves planning time if you teach a different grade level in the future.

5. Select the category you will teach first. Combine any concepts that are appropriate to teach together and arrange the concepts using any or all of the following criteria:

    ◆ obvious chronological, sequential, ascending, descending order, etc.

    ◆ availability of materials

    ◆ your teaching style

6. Organize the binder according to the organization of your unit. In your binder, divide each unit into categories and label each concept. For example, a unit on grammar might be divided by the different parts of speech: adjectives, adverbs, verbals, etc. Use colored tabs for main categories and clear tabs for sub-divisions of each.

7. Locate teaching materials for each concept by searching through your list of cross-reference enrichment materials (see pages 78–81) and checking with the school or district media specialist for additional sources. Include all materials gathered that might relate to the concept (it is easier to discard or return materials than to relocate them again). Because students' needs will change from class to class, it is a good idea to keep a wide variety of materials on hand. Keep a running list of your favorites.

8. Copy information, worksheets, and answer keys when possible so that the original pages are always left intact within the book. (You may want to locate the material at a later date and might forget that you filed it in a particular unit.) Always copy answer sheets and clip them directly to the appropriate worksheet. Whenever possible, write

answers directly on an extra copy of the student's worksheet. It is much easier to answer questions when you can see the original assignment. Be sure to observe copyright laws.

9. Organize and file materials by concept. Use color coding wherever possible.

10. Place a copy of the unit lesson plan worksheet (page 65) at the beginning of each concept section in your binder.

11. Complete the unit lesson plan worksheet, including the concept, objectives, and expected student outcomes. (See "Sample Unit Lesson Plan," page 64.) You may choose to complete this after Step 13 below. While you should not spend a great deal of time on this, it is worth some effort as it helps you focus your objectives and provides for realistic and specific learning activities and outcomes.

12. Review all materials gathered for each concept and list the ones you will actually use on the unit lesson plan worksheet.

13. Brainstorm and review various teaching approaches and activities that best suit your students, materials, objectives, and outcomes. (Refer to "Using Learning Styles in the Classroom," page 39.)

   ◆ Include a wide variety of materials for all learning and sensory modalities.

   ◆ Plan a wide variety of teaching approaches, such as minilectures, full lectures, games, student-initiated activities, discussions, group and individual presentations, and manipulative materials.

   ◆ To increase attention span, always remember to include at least 2 different activities in the lesson plan for each class period. (For example, combine a minilecture with a game, or a hands-on activity with a written exercise.)

   ◆ Plan appropriate time to present clear directions for the assignment.

   ◆ Allow 2–4 minutes for student questions and 1–2 minutes for student entries in a class summary log (see pages 218–221).

   ◆ When appropriate, plan an opportunity for students to apply the newly learned concept in some way before leaving the classroom.

14. Write step-by-step learning activities. For additional reference, see the sample unit lesson plan on page 64.

   ◆ Use chronological order.

   ◆ Include time estimates per activity. Share these estimates with students when giving the assignment.

UNIT PLAN SUGGESTIONS

◆ Be specific enough to include all necessary details.

◆ Be general enough not to waste time writing excessive material.

◆ Number the steps for quick referral.

◆ Allow time for a summary of concept(s).

15. Review the lesson plans and activities. Decide how much time each will take and jot it down in the appropriate column. This will help you know whether you will need to teach a concept in one day or over a series of days.

ADDITIONAL SUGGESTIONS

◆ Number each page of your lesson plan for easy reference.

◆ Label the unit binder on the front cover and the spine for easy recognition.

BRIEF CURRICULUM GUIDE ACROSS THREE GRADE LEVELS
Language Arts

VOCABULARY DEVELOPMENT

Grade 7	Grade 8	Grade 9
prefixes	acronyms	compound words
suffixes	heteronyms	synonyms
roots (Latin, Greek)	eponyms	antonyms
word usage (affect/effect, etc.)	syllabication	prefixes
	affixes	suffixes
homonyms, synonyms	etymologies	analogies
antonyms	dialects	roots (Latin)

GRAMMAR/SENTENCE SKILLS

Grade 7	Grade 8	Grade 9
subject/verb agreement	prepositional phrases	subordinate conjunction
define and recognize:	sentence patterns (S+V+O)	complex sentences
• nouns	direct objects	verbals:
• verbs	sentence structure	• gerunds
• pronouns	define and recognize:	• participles
• adjectives	• simple	• infinitives
• adverbs	• compound	clauses:
• prepositions	• complex	• adjective
• conjunctions	independent/dependent	• adverb
• interjections	clauses	• noun
complete/simple predicates	pronoun/antecedent	functional shift
sentence types	agreement	transitions
• interrogative	verb tenses	phrases
• declarative	verb types	• appositive
• imperative		• verbal
appositive		

MECHANICS

Grade 7	Grade 8	Grade 9
capitalization	abbreviations	colon
commas	quotation marks	dash/hyphen
periods	underlining	brackets
exclamation points	italics	apostrophe
question marks	apostrophe	brace
parenthesis	plurals	special plurals (e.g. deer)
apostrophe	spelling rules	spelling
spelling rules	misused homonyms	• doubling final
misused homonyms	pronoun reference	consonants
proper paragraphing	• people	• "e" endings
sentence skills	• objects	misused homonyms
• run-ons	• animals	misplaced modifiers
• fragments		
• sentence combining		

EXPOSITIONAL TYPES AND ELEMENTS

Grade 7	Grade 8	Grade 9
paragraph composition	types of composition	business letters
main ideas	• definition	research paper
support details	• explanation	thesis
topic sentence	• persuasion	précis
conclusion	• information	transitional forms
the writing process steps	• description	paragraphs and longer essays
creative writing	• narration	parallel construction
paraphrasing	paragraphs and longer essays	unity
summarizing	introduction	coherence
main ideas	conclusion	creative writing
supporting details	arrangement of details by:	sequencing
cause/effect	• chronological order	skimming
sequence	• spatial order	scanning
plot	• order of importance	analyzing
setting	creative writing	• newspaper
characterization		• magazines
		• drama
		• film/photographs

GENRE

Grade 7	Grade 8	Grade 9
short story	mythology	short story
poetry	folklore	poetry
drama	novel	drama
novel	essay	novel
essay		essay

REFERENCE SKILLS

Grade 7	Grade 8	Grade 9
library reference skills:	library reference skills:	library reference skills:
• library catalog	• information gathering	• integration of all materials
• parts of the library	locational skills:	locational skills
locational skills:	• Reader's Guide	format:
• table of contents	• specialized encyclopedias	• transitions
• preface	format:	• paragraph development
• appendix	• introduction	• topic sentences
• dictionary	• conclusion	• supporting details
• thesaurus	research paper	• special purpose paragraph
• almanac	(to be included in an appropriate speech/paper):	expanded research paper:
format:	• 3 references	• 4 references
• thesis statements	• 5 or more direct references	• 7 direct references
• parenthetical reference (MLA)		
• documentation (footnotes)		
bibliography		

LITERARY FORMS AND DEVICES

Grade 7	Grade 8	Grade 9
plot	dialogue	imagery
setting	diction	parallelism
character	flashback	parody
theme	foreshadowing	soliloquy
point of view	imagery	exposition
climax	parable	dilemma
conflict	realism	static/dynamic
resolution	satire	characterization
symbolism	suspense	third person narrative
atmosphere	tone	omniscient
suspense	fantasy	action/reaction -
motivation	first person narrative	comparison and contrast
fact/opinion	literal	metaphor
inferences	figurative	personification
conclusion		hyperbole
connotation/denotation		consonance
cause/effect		assonance
imagery		rhyme patterns
alliteration		stanza
rhyme		traditional/contemporary
simile/metaphor		sonnet
onomatopoeia		ode
rhythm		

SPEECH

Grade 7	Grade 8		Grade 9
summarizing	types of speeches:	- assert specific	present speeches
paraphrasing	• debate	purpose of	critique speeches
sharing original	• demonstration	presentation	
work with others	• information	• body	
	• oral interpretation	- appropriate	
	• impromptu	organizational	
	• extemporaneous	methods	
	• persuasion	• conclusion	
	• propaganda	- summary	
	techniques	- call to action	
	speech techniques:	creating effective	
	• introductions	style/tone:	
	- creating audience	• pronunciation	
	interest through	• speed/enunciation	
	capture statements	• volume	
	- motivational	• gestures	
	strategies	• eye contact	
	- preview/overview		
	of content		

UNIT PLANNING OVERVIEW

Reproduce the calendars on the following pages as needed. Take a few moments to write in your unit plans for the school year for each class you teach. This will allow you to:

◆ plan the time limits per unit more realistically.

◆ see an outline of the course's general content.

◆ concentrate on the appropriate sequence of concepts for your source.

◆ visualize how all the units in all your classes fit together. (For example, if you have a difficult unit in one class, you may want to plan an easier one to teach concurrently in another class.)

◆ provide evidence of clear planning for administrators.

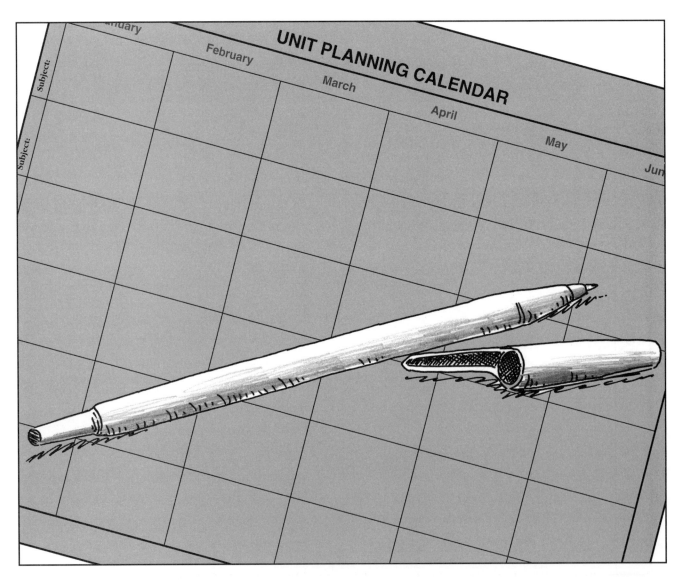

UNIT PLANNING CALENDAR

	January	February	March	April	May	June
Subject:						
Subject:						
Subject:						
Subject:						
Subject:						
Subject:						

UNIT PLANNING CALENDAR

	July	August	September	October	November	December
Subject:						
Subject:						
Subject:						
Subject:						
Subject:						
Subject:						

Teaching for Learning Success, Rev. Ed.

THE LUXURY VERSION

A sample detailed lesson plan is provided on the following page. It is called the luxury version because it is "loaded" with all of the extras. Consider using this format if your principal requires you to hand in complete lesson plans. It provides a great deal of security for beginning teachers, as it covers all aspects of a lesson. Writing specific objectives and student outcomes also helps to clarify the goals of the lesson. Use this lesson plan, as well, if you intend to share plans with another teacher, as it is well-organized and thorough.

Like a luxury car, this lesson plan will cost a little more . . . of your time.

SAMPLE UNIT LESSON PLAN

Unit: __Grammar__   Concepts: __Adjectives__

Total Time	Concept(s)	Materials	Objective(s)	Students Outcomes	Lesson Plans and Activities

45 min.	adjectives	- student blank paper
		- pen/pencil
		- 4 boxes of crackers or cookies
		- paper towels
		- Adjective worksheet
			- to identify adjectives within sentences
			- to use senses to identify and describe
			
			* objectives are what you want the student to learn in connection with the concept.
				- verbally define adjectives
				- write correct sentences containing adjectives
				- write advertising jingle using adjectives
				- speak in a group and orally use adjectives
				
				* Student outcomes are what the student actually produce (their product)
					1. Organize students into 4 groups.
					2. Tell students not to touch the box of crackers or cookies placed in the middle of their group.
					3. Students are to list words that describe the box as they see it (5 min.).
					4. Dump crackers/cookies on a paper towel; students look but do not touch the crackers/cookies.
					5. List words that now describe how the crackers/cookies look (5 min.).
					6. Each student takes handful of crackers/cookies from paper towel and tastes, smells, and feels crackers/cookies (2 min.).
					7. Make another list of words that describes the crackers (5 min.)
					8. Have students help create a definition of adjectives; write on board.
					9. In groups, write a 1 min. TV commercial for these crackers: (5 min.):
					  - group writes 1 script
					  - use words from lists
					10. Group gives short oral presentation of advertisement (15 min.).
					11. Distribute, explain, and work first three sentences on the worksheet (4-5 min.).
					12. Fill in class summary logs (5 min.).

Teaching for Learning Success, Rev. Ed.

UNIT LESSON PLAN

Unit: _____   Concepts: _____

Total Time	Concept(s)	Materials	Objective(s)	Students Outcomes	Lesson Plans and Activities

THE MIDSIZE VERSION

As with a midsize car, the sample lesson plan form on the following page contains adequate details, but is not fancy. Consider using this lesson plan if you feel comfortable leaving a few gaps in your planning (especially if you have taught the subject before) and know the basic concepts and elements of the lesson.

The midsize lesson plan will not take as much of your time to complete, or contain as many details, as the luxury version.

Teaching for Learning Success, Rev. Ed.

LESSON PLANS

Unit:_____ Concepts: _____

Materials	Objectives	Lesson Plans and Activities

THE COMPACT VERSION

The lesson plan form on the following page contains very few details. Use this lesson plan if you have taught this course before and feel comfortable with a brief list of the subject's main concepts. You should be familiar with all of the "basics" of the subject.

This lesson plan will not take much of your time to complete and, like a compact car, does not contain many details, but it is quite adequate for the experienced teacher.

Teaching for Learning Success, Rev. Ed.

LESSON PLANS

Unit:_____	Concepts: _____
Materials	**Lesson Plans and Activities**

LESSON PLAN CHECKLIST

Did you remember to:

❑ check the curriculum guide?

❑ check through all enrichment materials available?

❑ use a multimedia approach when appropriate?

❑ include all learning styles?
  - left-brain dominant
  - right-brain dominant
  - auditory modality
  - visual modality
  - kinesthetic modality

❑ vary the activities?
  - independent work
  - small-group work
  - large-group work
  - quiet work
  - active work

❑ provide for active learning?

❑ create and administer a pretest?

❑ involve students in the planning and evaluating process, if appropriate?

❑ include creative attention grabbers at the beginning of lessons?

❑ sequence concepts so that each concept and skill level builds on the previous one?

❑ discuss with students why they need to learn the concepts and information and how they can use and transfer the information?

❑ include specific study skills that help students learn the information?

❑ adjust the rate of learning to suit all students and plan enough time for the unit to meet all learning rates?

❑ include class time for students to practice successful study skills such as weekly vocabulary reviews, daily summary logs, and test review discussions?

❑ create some form of evaluation such as a test or a final project?

❑ _____

❑ _____

❑ _____

❑ _____

❑ _____

PREPARING FOR A SUBSTITUTE

A Word About Your Substitute

1. Discuss classroom rules at the beginning of the year, include specific expectations for student behavior in the presence of a substitute teacher. Inform students that you will reinforce any disciplinary measures taken by the substitute.

2. If some form of disciplinary action was taken by the substitute, always reinforce it or follow through with it unless you feel that the action was completely inappropriate.

3. When preparing for a substitute, write lesson plans that continue the regular flow of your classes. However, if your plans are quite involved and require special preparation, consider a different activity suitable to the content.

4. If you return to your class to find that your plans were not carried out as instructed, do not criticize the substitute teacher in front of your students. If the substitute made serious errors, inform your principal and contact the substitute office to request that the substitute not be assigned to your classroom in the future.

5. If you return to your class to find that everything went very well, be sure to request that substitute teacher again. Personally contact the substitute and give him or her positive feedback. Try to find at least two substitutes upon whom you can depend. It is much easier for both your students and for the substitute teacher if the he or she is familiar with your expectations and classroom management style.

6. When you can plan ahead for a substitute, tell your students who is coming, review your expectations again, and mention that you look forward to hearing a wonderful report from your friend (the substitute) about their cooperative behavior. Remind students that their behavior reflects not only on themselves and their teacher, but on the school as a whole.

Lesson Plans

If you know ahead of time that you need to leave the classroom, arrange well in advance for your favorite substitute. Discuss lesson plans at that time if the substitute will need to read background information to prepare for your class. Having a substitute who is familiar with your routines and rules is an asset.

The lesson plans you develop for the day(s) you will be absent should be simple and organized so that they can be easily understood by the substitute teacher. Consider using the same format each time you need a substitute; this will make the task of organizing for a substitute's arrival easier. Your regular substitute will also benefit from the consistency of the format. The daily lesson plan form on page 76 provides an organized and easy-to-read reproducible master lesson plan. Use this form in conjunction with the general information form on pages 74–75. Always keep an adequate supply of daily lesson plan forms on hand for immediate use. Keep several blank copies at home in case you need to have someone deliver plans to your school.

Always keep backup lesson plans on hand for those true emergencies when you cannot formulate a daily plan. Develop a backup lesson plan using the form on page 77 for each course that you teach. The backup plan should be an enrichment activity rather than an activity based on a specific unit or concept idea, and may include group activities, games, or independent reading assignments that can be easily initiated by a substitute teacher and completed by the students. The location of these plans should be noted in your substitute folder with the stipulation that they are to be used only if regular plans are not available. Consider keeping the backup plans in a file other than the substitute folder to avoid any possibility of confusion with the regular daily plan you provide.

Organizing Your Substitute Folder

1. Most schools keep individual file folders in the main office to give to substitute teachers when they check in for the day. Be sure to update these folders as changes in district, building, and personal policies occur.

2. Keep in your personal phone directory at home (or written on a separate 3" x 5" index card taped in a conspicuous location) the substitute office phone number and several names and phone numbers of good substitutes. Clearly label them and keep this information together in an obvious place in your directory so that another person can arrange for a substitute in case you are unable to do it for yourself. Remember, if you always plan for the unexpected, it is less likely to happen.

3. Every substitute folder should be well organized and contain the following (Consider organizing this into major categories with colored tabs. For example, General Substitute Information, Location of Materials, Specific Classes, etc.):

   ◆ building floor plans

   ◆ emergency steps for fire and bomb threat evacuation drills, with appropriate exit doors marked on the floor plan

   ◆ school policies and specific rules

   ◆ a list of members of the administration and faculty with corresponding office and/or classroom numbers

   ◆ daily class and lunch schedule; bell schedule

   ◆ your team teachers' names or the name of the most helpful teacher nearest your classroom

   ◆ list of 2–3 dependable and helpful students in each class

◆ list of students with special needs

- medical problems or physical disabilities and limitations

- learning disabilities

- highly gifted

- serious discipline concerns

◆ your home phone number or where you can be reached, if possible

◆ important procedures (attendance, discipline, lunch count, etc.)

◆ location of important materials (texts, seating charts, etc.)

◆ location of labeled folder for Switch game handouts (see pages 287–288)

◆ information on how to collect and return student papers

◆ a brief explanation of your grading system

◆ extra copies of necessary blank forms (attendance, hall passes, etc.)

◆ a copy of your classroom policies (same one used with students and parents at the beginning of the year)

The form on pages 74–75 contains each of the above categories. It is ready to be reproduced and filled in with the appropriate information. You will need only one copy to include in your permanent substitute folder. Remember to change any information as needed.

GENERAL INFORMATION FOR THE SUBSTITUTE

*This is basic information for my classes for the year. Specific information as it pertains to certain classes or the particular day you are teaching will be included in the daily lesson plan section.

Teacher's Name _____ **Home Phone** _____

Copy Machine _____ **Helpful Teacher** _____ **Room** _____

DAILY SCHEDULE

Period	Time	Room	1st Semester/2nd Semester Classes
_____	____ — ____	_____	_____
_____	____ — ____	_____	_____
_____	____ — ____	_____	_____
_____	____ — ____	_____	_____
_____	____ — ____	_____	_____
_____	____ — ____	_____	_____
_____	____ — ____	_____	_____
_____	____ — ____	_____	_____

SPECIAL STUDENTS

Period	Helpful Students	Health Concerns, etc.	Discipline Concerns	Special Needs Students
_____	_____			
_____	_____			
_____	_____			
_____	_____			
_____	_____			
_____	_____			

Students Excused from Class for Special Reasons:

_____

_____

_____

_____

_____

Teaching for Learning Success, Rev. Ed.

Location of Materials and Procedures: *(Additional specific information may be included on separate daily plans.)*

1. Seating Chart and Attendance Forms: _____

_____

2. Discipline Procedure: _____

_____

3. Textbooks:_____

_____

4. Collecting Student Papers:_____

_____

5. Returning Student Papers:_____

_____

6. Handouts: _____

_____

7. "Switch Game" Handouts:_____

_____

8. Emergency Lesson Plans: _____

_____

9. Gradebook: _____

_____

10. _____

_____

In case of an emergency, and I am unable to leave lesson plans, backup lesson plans for each class that may be used are:

_____

_____

_____

_____

_____

Items also located in this folder:

- ◆ building floor plans
- ◆ fire/bomb emergency exits
- ◆ school policies
- ◆ list of administration and faculty members

- ◆ _____
- ◆ _____
- ◆ _____

Notes:

_____

_____

_____

_____

DAILY LESSON PLAN

Date _____

Teacher's Name _____

Substitute's Name _____

* Please read "General Information for the Substitute" in this folder.
It contains important basic material pertinent to all classes today.

Period: _____ Time: _____ Class: _____ Room: _____

Absent: _____

Substitute's Notes: _____
_____
_____
_____
_____

Period: _____ Time: _____ Class: _____ Room: _____

Absent: _____

Substitute's Notes: _____
_____
_____
_____
_____

Teaching for Learning Success, Rev. Ed.

BACKUP LESSON PLAN

Teacher's Name _____

Substitute's Name _____

* Please read "General Information for the Substitute" in this folder. It contains important basic material pertinent to all classes. Due to an emergency, I was unable to prepare regular plans for you today. Please follow the plans below for every class. Inform students that all regular plans for today will be suspended until tomorrow. Additional materials are located in

_____

Period: _____ Time: _____ Class: _____ Room: _____

Absent: _____

Substitute's Notes: _____

_____

_____

_____

_____

Period: _____ Time: _____ Class: _____ Room: _____

Absent: _____

Substitute's Notes: _____

_____

_____

_____

_____

MATERIALS AT YOUR FINGERTIPS
—————— Creating a Cross-reference ——————
of Enrichment Materials

WHAT

A cross-reference of enrichment materials is an invaluable, organized resource list that cross-references all of your teaching materials according to specific subject area concepts. Add to it every year whenever you acquire new materials.

WHY

Using a cross reference of enrichment materials:

◆ saves time by providing quick-and-easy access to all materials at once.

◆ provides an organized method of finding just the right item for a class or student with special needs.

◆ makes you more familiar with all of your enrichment materials.

◆ eliminates comments such as: "I wish I had found this last month when I was teaching. . . " and "I forgot I had this!"

◆ reinforces organizational skills for successful teaching.

◆ allows you to locate immediately all available materials and makes unit and lesson planning much easier.

◆ allows the most flexibility for maximizing use of materials and references.

MATERIALS

You will need:

◆ time (This is a time-consuming effort. It is well worth the time spent, however, as it will continue to save you a lot of time for years to come!),

◆ multiple copies of the reproducible cross-reference form (see page 81),

◆ three-ring binder (allows for additions and deletions),

◆ colored plastic tabs or paper dividers with colored tabs to label the different concepts and units,

◆ district or school curriculum guide.

Teaching for Learning Success, Rev. Ed.

HOW

- List the units and specific concepts for each across the top of the form. Use a separate page for each main unit and allow space or extra pages for future additions.

- Three-hole punch all papers.

- Prepare colored tabs or paper dividers with tabs by labeling each with a main unit of study. Place the appropriate tabs or dividers where necessary to label main units.

- Use clear plastic labels to subdivide information when needed.

- Place all papers inside the binder.

- Briefly scan each resource you plan to use, decide on its appropriate use, and add it to the materials list. It is easier to take one resource, page by page, and enter it in the various pages of the form. In the grid, include the page number on which the concepts can be found.

- Regularly make the time to add to your cross-reference file any new materials you purchase.

SUGGESTIONS

- On separate pages, list the materials by title and include the author, publisher, publication date, ISBN number, and any other pertinent information. This data will make it easy to replace any lost or missing materials. Place these pages in the back of the binder.

- Number all of the pages in the binder (including the blank forms) and make a table of contents for quick access to specific concepts. Place these pages in the front of the binder.

- Remember: it is much easier to keep up than catch up. The time you make to enter all appropriate information from new materials immediately when you obtain it will save you more hours hunting for it in the future!

CROSS-REFERENCE MATERIALS
(Sample)

UNIT __Short stories__

MATERIALS	CONCEPTS	THEME	PLOT	CLIMAX	RESOLUTION
Coronado Text		16	16	18	22
Crosswords Content		7			
Short Stories, Inc.				36	37

CROSS-REFERENCE MATERIALS

UNIT _____ / MATERIALS	CONCEPTS	THEME	PLOT	CLIMAX	RESOLUTION																			

Teaching for Learning Success, Rev. Ed.

ORGANIZING A GRADEBOOK

Refer to the sample gradebook on pages 84–85 as you read through the following information.

1. Enter students' names after the drop/add date or as soon as you think permanent enrollment has been achieved. Grades and points can be kept on graph paper until enrollment stabilizes.

2. Write your name, address, and phone number on the inside of your gradebook in case of loss. Write your name and the school's name on the book's outside cover.

3. Complete your daily class schedule and any other regular time schedules as needed.

4. Divide your gradebook for the entire year in such a way that provides for the least amount of recopying. Before copying class lists in your gradebook, consider the length of the classes (are they quarter, semester, or yearlong classes?). For example, if you have 5 yearlong classes and there are 25 pages available in your gradebook, allow five pages for the first class, the next 5 pages for the second class, and so on. Staple together the first five pages, the next 5 together, etc., so that when you turn the page to record grades in one class they will all turn at once. At the end of the first quarter, simply fold over the left side of the next empty page so that the names of the original list align with the empty pages. Restaple each set of pages.

5. Attach colored plastic tabs labeled with the period or class name to your gradebook. This provides quick access when referring to or recording grades.

6. Use the top header space for assignment number and due date.

7. Before deciding whether to double or single space student names, allow space at the bottom of the page to write the titles of assignments and the points possible for each assignment. This will save time if you plan to reenter the grades on a computer.

8. Allow space in the last column on the right-hand page to record extra credit points, if you use them.

9. Allow a column for midterm and final grades, if appropriate. Even if you have a class printout of grades, this will save time as you will have all of the pertinent information in one place.

10. Number the spaces to the right of the spiral or binding on the right-hand page to match those of the original student list. Often, the lines on the pages do not match up, and this will prevent grades from being incorrectly recorded.

11. Every 2–3 weeks, photocopy your gradebook in case of loss. Keep the copies in a file. Every 1-2 weeks, transfer grades to your computer grade software to keep current.

12. Decide whether you will allow students to refer to your gradebook under your supervision or if they are not to have access to it. Share this decision with students early in the course. Make a note of your policy in the substitute folder in an easily visible location.

13. Use a pencil to record grades in progress (assignments that may be rewritten for a better grade, etc.). When the assignment has been completed, record the final grade in ink.

14. Write a simple explanation of your grading system and keep it in your files. Make a copy of it and attach it to the gradebook by stapling it to the back of the last page or taping it on the inside of the back cover. This information can be invaluable if a teacher must assume your role for any reason. Be sure to include this information in the substitute folder.

15. If you develop a special system for recording grades, such as a dot in the corner of a square where a grade appears, or a square penned around a certain grade, be sure to write a key to your code and keep it in the front of your gradebook so that another teacher will be able to continue your system if necessary. Also, school policy may dictate that you leave your gradebook with your principal at the end of the year in order that students' grades may be examined in your absence.

16. When choosing grade/record-keeping computer software, consider the flexibility you will need to add information on pages 84–85.

SAMPLE GRADEBOOK

Subject... *8th L.A.*

Section *Period 6*

Student Number	Students	Due Date →		1st week					2nd week					3rd week					4th week					5th week				
			9/7	9/10	9/14	9/20	9/23	9/25	10/1	10/3	10/6	10/11																
	Assignment #		1	2	3	4	5		6	7	8	9	10															
	Students		M	T	W	T	F		M	T	W	T	F		M	T	W	T	F		M	T	W	T	F		M	T	W	T	F
1	Abbott, Alice		9	13	29	5	5		30																			
2																												
3	Babcock, Ted		■	14	21	5	4		29																			
4																												
5	Campbell, Ed		10	3	26	4	5		30																			
6																												
7	Cody, Eli		6	15	27	5	5		■																			
8																												
9	Frost, Rachel		7	11	□20	5	4		26																			
10																												
11																												
12																												
13																												
14																												
15																												
16																												
17																												
18																												
19																												
20																												
21	Possible #Points →		10	15	30	5	5		30																			
22																												
23	KEY:																											
24																												
25	■ = voucher																											
26	□ = rewrite																											
27		Assignment Titles	Worksheet #4	L.A.B. Notes	L.A.B. Summary	Pop Quiz #1	Pop Quiz #2		Chapter Test 2																			
28																												
29																												
30																												

Teaching for Learning Success, Rev. Ed.

SAMPLE GRADEBOOK

Due Date	6th week					7th week					8th week					9th week										Mid Term Gr.	Final Gr.		Extra Credit							Summary			E.C. Totals
	M	T	W	T	F	M	T	W	T	F	M	T	W	T	F	M	T	W	T	F																		
1																												2	1	3			1				
2																																	2				
3																												1	2				3				
4																																	4				
5																												3	2	1			5				
6																																	6				
7																												1	1	1			7				
8																																	8				
9																													2				9				
10																																	10				
11																																	11				
12																																	12				
13																																	13				
14																																	14				
15																																	15				
16																																	16				
17																																	17				
18																																	18				
19																																	19				
20																																	20				
21																																	21				
22																																	22				
23																																	23				
24																																	24				
25																																	25				
26																																	26				
27																																	27				
28																																	28				
29																																	29				
30																																	30				

GRADING PAPERS:
Making It Easier

If students are to learn, they must be motivated to produce work. With hundreds of students producing work each day, however, this adds up to a great deal of time spent grading. Grading papers is not always the easiest or most enjoyable part of a teacher's busy day. Furthermore, your class load may be so large that it may not be possible for you to grade every student's paper all of the time.

Assistance is available in a variety of forms: peer grading in class, student scan sheets, teacher's aids, student assistants, parent volunteers, etc. Decide how much and which types of assignments you want to grade and which ones you feel comfortable allowing others to grade. Each teacher has a different philosophy concerning grading procedures and will usually choose a combination of grading tactics that best suit his or her teaching style and student needs.

Review the following ideas and suggestions that were designed to give the busy teacher a boost when grading papers. You may want to combine or adapt to your own style any suggestions that seem appropriate for your classroom.

Rewrite Policy

Written assignments are given to students to improve their learning and retention. A student learns more when given the opportunity to correct errors. Consider establishing a rewrite or re-do policy that allows students to correct errors made in the original assignment and hand the assignment in again and again until judged acceptable by both student and teacher. The final copy would then replace the original copy in the student's writing portfolio and/or receive additional points or a better grade. Set a deadline for all rewrites and a standard for corrections.

When recording grades, document the completion of the first paper in pencil or a specific color of type. Once the assignment has been rewritten and regraded, record the final grade in pen or a different color in the computer.

You may choose specific assignments to be rewritten throughout the course/year or make your rewrite policy applicable to every assignment. Discuss your rewrite policy when giving directions to students regarding any assignment. Consider making specific suggestions on student papers or circling errors but not adding the right answer. This forces the student to think of the better/correct answer and not just recopy your suggestions or corrections. See "Teacher-Graded Papers" on page 87.

Teaching for Learning Success, Rev. Ed.

Teacher-Graded Papers

Consider using green instead of red ink. Green ink is used less in grading than red ink and, therefore, not as commonly associated with negative feelings.

Develop a code to use in the margins of papers to signal errors in paragraph style or grammar, specific math answers, etc. Students learn more when they must locate an error themselves than if misspelled words are circled or correct punctuation is inserted for them. Create your own code, or use the one suggested below. Be sure to write the code for the error on the line in which the error occurs. For example, one "sp" signals to the student that there is one spelling error on that line of writing. "sp, sp" or "2sp" on the same line signals that there are two spelling errors on that line. Any combination of coded errors may appear on one line in the margin. Make copies of your writing code and distribute to each student. Post one on a bulletin board, as well. Consider including a copy in your substitute folder if you expect the substitute to correct papers.

Sample Code:

sp *spelling error*

g *grammar error*

ss *sentence structure (confusing, poorly constructed)*

wc *word choice (incorrect use of a word, wrong homonym, choose better word to replace several poor ones)*

cs *combine sentences (too many short, choppy sentences; sentences need combining)*

ro *run-on sentence (sentence is too long; break it down)*

sm *see me (this correction requires further instruction; see the teacher for discussion)*

Teacher-Constructed and Graded Tests/Handouts

Have students use the symbols "+" for true and "0" for false on true/false assignments and tests. As these marks are easily distinguishable from each other, you can grade them much quicker than the more common "t/f" true/false tests. Students also cannot try to make an answer look both true and false. Clearly write these directions on each handout or test section and then stick to the system—to not be tempted to accept T/F answers!

When writing tests, design an answer column on either the left- or right-hand margin. Then, when you correct the tests, place four or five papers on top of each other in a staggered line, revealing only the answer columns. Place the answer key beneath and to the left of the stack of papers and glance at all of the papers at once. Consider using a slash (/) rather than a check (√).

GRADING PAPERS

Construct multiple choice or true/false tests with separate answer sheets. Create the answer sheets with matching item numbers and appropriately labeled circles for each question. For example:

	A	B	C	D			true	false
1.	0	0	0	0		1.	0	0
2.	0	0	0	0		2.	0	0

Students are instructed to fill in the correct circles to answer the questions. Construct an answer sheet by punching a hole in the correct location on the piece of acetate. Place the acetate answer sheet on top of the students' tests for easy grading. Simply fill in the circles with colored ink.

Peer Grading in Class

Grading papers in class can not only save hours of work for teachers, but can be a terrific learning experience for students as well. Assignments that require a great deal of subjective decision making are not appropriate for peer grading, however. ALWAYS check with district and building policy to be certain this is permissible.

If you are using green ink to correct and grade assignments, have students use red pencils when correcting papers. You can quickly distinguish between your marks in green and those of your students in red.

Students may choose with whom they wish to exchange papers, or you can assign grading partners. One problem with the policy of allowing friends to exchange papers is the possibility of cheating. Be aware of this, and be observant. Have a solution to this problem on-hand should it arise, and be prepared to enforce it.

Before correcting papers in class, always state your expectations, the point system for that particular assignment, and any other specific instructions. Insist on everyone's attention and say the directions only once. Condition your class early in the year to listen carefully to directions. Having to repeat directions when correcting papers in class can consume a great deal of class time.

Consider establishing a policy to deal with students who are not prepared with a completed assignment when it is time to exchange papers. There will always be some students who insist on being given extra time to complete their assignments before papers are exchanged. Remember, when giving the original directions for the assignment, clearly state the exact due date and class time.

Always have students sign their names in red ink at the top of the papers they have graded. Do not allow initials, and consider a specific location, such as the upper right or left corner.

Whenever possible, display the answer key on the overhead projector to allow students to have something to view while listening to the answers. This greatly helps visual as well as auditory learners!

Teaching for Learning Success, Rev. Ed.

It is helpful to write the final grading scale on the board or on an overhead transparency to allow students to recheck it before writing the grade or points on the paper.

Before beginning an in-class grading session, give students instruction on how to:

- mark an incorrect answer (circle it, write a mark through it, use a check mark next to it)
- mark a correct answer (leave it alone, write a "c" beside it)
- write the grade at the top (percentage correct, number of correct points over number of possible points, number of incorrect points over number of possible points, a letter grade)
- place the grade on the top of the paper in a specific location
- sign the paper they are grading and where to put their signature

Paraprofessionals or Adult Classroom Aids and Volunteers

Write out your expectations and special instructions or procedures so that they can refer to them without interrupting you while you are teaching. Place a copy of these instructions in your substitute folder.

Take a few moments to review your instructions with them. They will feel better about doing just what you expect, and you will feel more confident, too.

If a parent volunteer has a child in your class, ask whether he or she feels comfortable grading his or her own child's assignments and tests. Do you, as the teacher, feel comfortable? What is your policy on this subject?

Provide a suitable place for your assistants and volunteers to correct papers. If they work in the classroom while students are present, inform students not to visit with them or check to see if their papers have been corrected. Do not allow any volunteers, aids, or student helpers to take papers home.

Decide if you are comfortable allowing aids and volunteers to record grades in the gradebook or on a computer.

Student Aids

Know how competent the student is before turning over papers to be graded. Some student aids are extremely capable and others would better serve you by completing other tasks. Decide whether this student would be fair if grading a friend's paper or test.

Write out any instructions for grading papers. Thoroughly discuss your expectations and particular rules. Include this information in the section for paraprofessionals or adult classroom aids and volunteers and place it in your substitute folder.

Decide if you are comfortable allowing student aids to grade tests or to enter grades in your gradebook or on a computer. Do you feel that it is appropriate for student aids to have access to other students' grades?

GRADING PAPERS

A Few Final Notes About Grading

Strive to return graded student papers within 1–3 days. "Old" graded papers lose their teaching value when returned to students—the only thing they will relate to is their name on the paper.

Your written comments on a paper mean more than a grade at the top. Be positive. **You can be positively critical! Remember to "hide" the grade in your comments to force them to read what you write!**

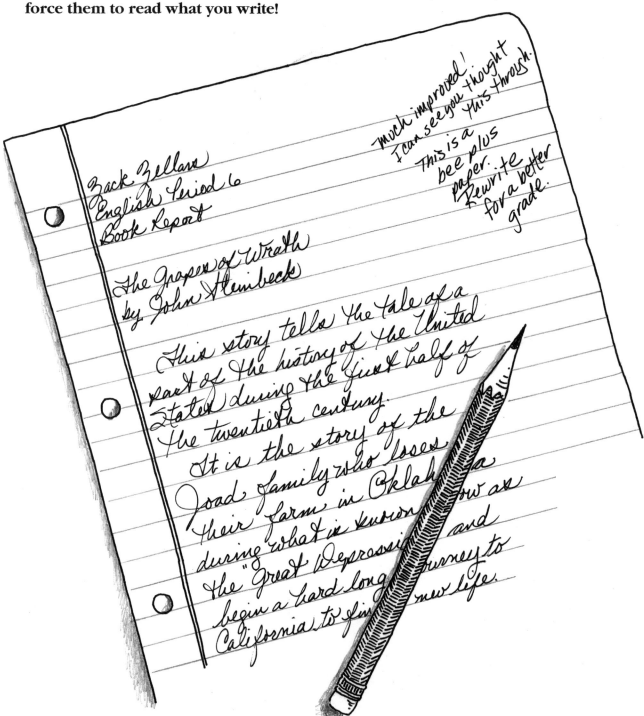

GIVING DIRECTIONS

So much in teaching cannot be handled with formulas; however, giving directions is different. If you follow this set of rules, you will find that your students will understand more clearly what you want them to do, and you will not be asked to repeat directions more than once.

1. Insist on everyone's quiet and undivided attention. Check for good eye contact from all students. Make it clear to your students that you give directions only once. Inform students that they will need to write down your instructions if they are not on the handout.

2. Clearly and slowly state your instructions, introducing them step by step. If there are more than three steps to follow, write them on the board or on a transparency.

3. Demonstrate a strategy that might be used to complete the assignment. Review any special thinking strategies required.

4. Give an example or do the first problem with students to get them started.

5. List all materials needed for the assignment.

6. State an approximate amount of time it should take to complete the assignment well.

7. State the assignment's due date, write it on the calendar, and give students time to write it on their assignment calendars. Be specific: first or last part of the class, etc.

8. Briefly discuss why students need to learn this information and how it can be applied in the future.

9. Ask one student to quickly repeat or summarize the assignment.

10. Ask for questions, allowing at least 30 seconds for students to think of any.

IN BRIEF

1. Get student attention

2. Give directions

3. Demonstrate strategy

4. Give examples

5. List materials

6. Estimate time

7. State due date and time

8. Discuss why and how

9. Student summary

10. Student questions

SUGGESTIONS FOR CREATING HANDOUTS AND TESTS

These tips are designed to help you produce handouts, overhead transparencies, and tests that are more appealing and successful for students. There are a number of ways teachers can make the information on handouts and tests more meaningful to students, easier and quicker to learn, and retained longer. Consider some of these tips the next time you are preparing a paper or a test.

1. Always leave adequate space for the student's name at the top of a paper and the first page of a multiple-page handout or test.

   Many times, a student forgets to put his or her name on a paper if there is no name line available.

2. Always leave adequate space near the top of the page for placement of comments and grade or score.

3. Include at least one graphic on every page for visual interest.

4. Be aware of the overall use of space.

   ◆ Do not clutter a page with information. This makes it distracting and confusing.

   ◆ Always group together related information and leave ample space between separate concepts.

   ◆ Leave sufficient margins on all four sides of the page.

   ◆ Use both fronts and backs of paper for tests, if possible.

5. When presenting main topics, subtopics, and details, always indent the material to demonstrate how the information is related.

   Use a bullet or some other signal to readily identify information as being separate. For example, you may want to follow an outline format like this:

   ### MAIN TOPIC
   - Supporting Idea
   - Supporting Idea
   - Supporting Idea
       - *detail*
       - *example*
   - Supporting Idea
       - *detail*

Teaching for Learning Success, Rev. Ed.

6. A page on which information is presented in paragraphs is more difficult to understand and more time-consuming to read than one on which the information has been organized into:

   ◆ lists

   ◆ columns

   ◆ shapes

   ◆ illustrations

   ◆ bulleted outlines

7. Consider all of the information you wish to include in the handout.

   Does it lend itself to a format that the mind can easily organize and store? For instance, if four main ideas, each having numerous subtopics and details, are presented, draw one vertical line down the middle of the paper (from the top margin to the bottom margin) and one horizontal line across the middle of the paper (from the left margin to the right margin). This will create four rectangles that visually organize the information into four distinct categories. Create formats which best suit the available information. Refer to the section on graphic organizers (see pages 235–247) for additional ideas. Use these as listening guides for a lecture.

8. Use Roman numerals, numbers, capital letters, etc., only when necessary, as they tend to be distracting and are often unnecessary.

   Some students concentrate more on these symbols than the material being presented.

9. Use complete sentences only when necessary.

   Our minds more quickly pick up and retain short phrases (2–3 words) than complete sentences. Use and encourage students to use abbreviations and shorthand symbols.

10. Our minds remember colors (bright colors more than pastels), shapes, and placement—in that order.

    Keep this in mind when you create your next handout. Use graphic organizers to improve all that students are to learn and remember.

11. Use bright colors (not pastels) whenever possible on transparencies.

    Copy a handout onto a transparency and then use colors and shapes to highlight a block of information, vocabulary words, etc.

12. Be creative and use simple shapes wherever possible. Write a main concept inside a shape or draw a small shape to signal an important phrase.

13. Lines are very powerful and send strong visual signals to the mind.

    Use lines to set apart or join concepts and ideas.

SUGGESTIONS FOR CREATING HANDOUTS AND TESTS

14. Writing directions:

    ◆ Be very specific; leave no room for interpretation. Your directions might be perfectly clear to you, but not all students think like you do. Have someone else read your directions to make sure that they are easily and correctly understood.

    ◆ Give an example whenever possible.

    ◆ Use simple sentence structure.

    ◆ Use vocabulary familiar to all students.

    ◆ Do not give more than three commands written in one set of instructions.

    ◆ Instruct students to use the symbols "+" for true and "0" for false for any true/false statements; these symbols are easy to correct and cannot be easily confused.

    ◆ Incorporate a sense of humor into your handouts and tests.

15. Include 1 or 2 humorous items on a test. Laughter reduces anxiety and stress! Consider making every 15th (etc.) question a fun, easy, and humorous answer or choice.

16. Clearly label the points possible for each section or item on a test.

    Before beginning an exam, briefly discuss the test with your students. Point out any directions that might cause confusion, points possible for each section, typing errors, etc.

17. Try drawing horizontal lines to separate different segments on tests.

    The horizontal lines act as a signal to students to change their pattern of thinking, for example, when switching from a matching section to a true/false section.

18. When composing an essay test, leave enough space to write your own comments at the end of the student response. Be sure to include blank lines for student use. This makes correcting them much easier. Leave room for students to use a graphic organizer to map out their essay.

19. Leave room at the end of a handout or test for extra credit, if appropriate.

    Clearly label and separate an extra credit section with a line. Points possible should be very clearly marked, as well as how the extra points will be applied to the student's grade.

21. Word your questions carefully.

    Give appropriate information that will clarify answers if there is more than one possible answer. Have a colleague read your test for ambiguities.

22. For additional information on writing tests designed to be easily corrected, refer to the section on grading papers (pages 86–90).

Teaching for Learning Success, Rev. Ed.

BEGINNING-OF-THE-YEAR PRETEST

"Is a pretest really worth the time and effort?"

Absolutely! Not only does a pretest measure the abilities of individual students and the overall class level, but it helps students by giving them some idea of the focus of the course. A pretest clearly illustrates to students that while there are concepts they need to learn, they already know something about several of the content areas, linking the new information they need to learn with what they already know.

It also shows them that you care about how they feel concerning the subject and want to know their specific needs for the class. Offering students an opportunity to have an impact on how the class will be run can reverse some negative attitudes at the beginning of the year. Students feel respected and important if you include them in the planning process at every appropriate opportunity. By discussing some of your reasons for administering the test and how the results will help you plan the course, students realize that you are flexible and sensitive to their needs.

These tests can be invaluable to you throughout the entire course. As you begin to plan a new unit, for example, a review of the pretests can help you decide at which level to begin your instruction. These tests can also support you when and if parents or administrators question the level at which you are teaching certain concepts.

If you know before you begin a project where to start, the limitations and knowledge of your students, and have clearly defined goals, you will have a much better chance of succeeding as a teacher. A pretest can be an invaluable instrument for motivated and successful learning.

BEGINNING-OF-THE-YEAR PRETEST

WHAT

- ◆ A pretest is a nonthreatening, nongraded instrument given to all students during the first week of school.

- ◆ It is intended to assess students' knowledge and abilities in the course's main content areas.

WHY

- ◆ A pretest gives the teacher a general overview of how much each individual student (and the class as a whole) knows about a particular subject.

- ◆ It is a good instrument for assessing where to begin teaching a particular concept or subject.

- ◆ It provides students with an overview of the course and identifies to them the need to learn new information.

- ◆ A pretest provides parents and administrators with tangible evidence of student knowledge, abilities, and needs.

- ◆ A pretest helps the teacher to quickly identify any students working below or above their grade level.

- ◆ When returned to students at the end of the course, a pretest provides great positive reinforcement and tangible evidence of growth. It is usually a fun experience.

MATERIALS

You will need:

- ◆ a curriculum

- ◆ scan through ready-made pretests within your materials

- ◆ paper and pen or computer to write the pretest

- ◆ copy machine (to make copies of the test for students)

- ◆ a copy of the test on which to write specific comments regarding students' overall performance in each content area

- ◆ one labeled file folder per class in which to keep the tests until the end of the course

HOW

1. Review the main concepts of the curriculum to be covered.

2. Check for ready-made pretests in teacher guides or workbooks.

Teaching for Learning Success, Rev. Ed.

3. Create questions for each concept.

   Vary the format as certain students may have trouble working with particular formats. Use some of each of the following types of questions:

   ◆ true/false

   ◆ matching

   ◆ fill-in-the-blank

   ◆ multiple choice

   ◆ short answer

4. Always include an opportunity for the students to list:

   ◆ what they think are their strengths and weaknesses in this subject area

   ◆ what they like the most and least about this subject

   ◆ what they hope to gain from this course; what their goals are

5. The pretest should be constructed to be completed by students in one class period in order to give a true indication of each student's base of knowledge in a particular subject area. Do not allow students to talk with any other students, take tests out of the room, or take them home. All "make-up" tests should be done in class.

6. To do before distributing tests to students:

   ◆ Tell students why you think the test is important and how it will help you to better plan for their needs.

   ◆ Reassure them that the test will not count toward their grades in any way.

   ◆ Tell them you will keep the tests until the end of the course, at which time you will return them to allow the students to chart their progress.

7. Do not grade or mark incorrect responses. Have students do this on their own or go over correct answers when returning pretests as a review for the final test or after the final test for extra credit.

8. Quickly read through each test; use your copy of the test to make notes in each subject area for future reference.

   Helpful remarks include:

   ◆ the general performance level of responses per concept

   ◆ any tests with below-or above-grade-level responses

9. Make a list of priorities based on the test results.

10. File tests in a labeled file folder for the class/period.

   Refer to the section on suggestions for creating handouts and tests (pages 92–94) for more specifics on writing successful tests.

TEAM TEACHING

Team teaching is similar to planning and taking a vacation, and should be just as much fun. Although the travelers on a vacation bring with them their own ideas, agendas, expectations, and assorted luggage, they all manage to fit into the same car and arrive together. After all, they have the same destination.

It is important to respect and value your team members' differences. If you watch how other teachers teach, you will learn something new, and, undoubtedly, your team members will learn something new from you.

Suggestions and Tips

Listed below are suggestions to consider when in the planning stages of team teaching. Plan on meeting as a team several times before beginning your journey with students. Use portions of this list at each meeting to make sure you cover everything. Have fun and learn from each other!

1. When teaching with a team, expect, plan for, and celebrate the differences in every aspect of each team member's teaching style.

2. Always incorporate various student learning styles in every plan (see page 39).

3. Be willing to give 75% and expect 25% in return. If every team member does this, each will end up with 150% support.

4. If you do not know your team members very well, make time in your first planning session to get to know them and their teaching philosophy. Try for a first initial meeting over lunch at a favorite restaurant or potluck at a team member's house. You can appreciate another teacher more if you understand him or her as a person. Find out what is important to your team members in the areas of:

    ◆ student expectations

    ◆ teaching the whole child

    ◆ study skills

    ◆ learning concepts in curriculum areas

    ◆ memorizing information

    ◆ teaching to varied learning styles

    ◆ characteristics of a good learning atmosphere

    ◆ positive vs. negative feedback

- school/home communications

- common learning atmospheres for all students

- ability grouping

- grading papers

- timely return of assignments

- peer tutoring or mentoring

- group learning

- student assessment (teachers assessing students, students assessing other students, students assessing themselves, and students assessing teachers)

- particular strengths of each teacher

4. Agree on one set of discipline rules and a system for enforcing them with which everyone feels comfortable. This is very important.

5. Use master monthly calendars (page 135) and unit planning overview calendars (pages 61–62) when meeting to plan curriculum and lesson plans. Everyone needs to be coordinated.

6. Divide the generic tasks evenly among all team teachers to cut down the work load for everyone and to ensure that everything gets accomplished. Teachers can keep the same tasks for the entire year, or they can trade tasks at set times during the year. Keep in mind that some tasks are best completed by one person. All team members should touch base with each other regularly to assess whether their methods are successful or if modifications need to be made. Add your own ideas to this list of team tasks:

- writing, copying, and distributing the monthly, quarterly, or semester syllabus

- writing or posting daily agendas

- replenishing necessary student forms, handouts, and papers on the potpourri table (see page 146)

- replenishing necessary classroom supplies (tissues, chalk, pens, pencils, scratch paper, etc.)

- replenishing necessary teacher supplies (overhead transparency pens, correcting pens, file folders, etc.)

- watering plants

- posting completed assignments, activities, and information on the master student grade sheet

- making periodic copies of the gradebook or evaluation sheets

- changing weekly student assignments for classroom jobs
- writing thank-you letters to volunteers, parents, teachers, etc.
- changing bulletin boards
- writing or editing monthly parent newsletters (see pages 181–184)
- maintaining and photocopying the table of contents for weekly student take-home packets (see pages 187–189)
- writing daily assignments on the master calendar(s) (see page 133)
- providing treats for team meetings
- serving as a team representative to various committees, administrators, etc.
- checking in and out textbooks
- maintaining a substitute folder

7. Review school policies and decide on additional team policies (see pages 25–33).

8. Discuss how lesson plans are to be written. Each teacher can use an individual format or your team may decide to share a format. All team members should know where lesson plans, teacher's editions of textbooks, substitute binder or folder, and other shared materials are located.

9. Agree upon a systematic plan for keeping parents informed of and involved in your team's activities whenever appropriate.

10. Discuss the physical arrangement of the classroom(s) and teachers' offices. If necessary, plan for the location of traffic patterns, lab tables, learning station centers, reading corners, student reference centers, writing corners, etc.

11. Discuss bulletin boards and their uses, and decide which teacher is responsible for which bulletin board. Rotate on a monthly basis, content area basis, etc. Designate an appropriate, highly visual bulletin board on which to display permanent assignment calendars, announcements, student job lists, etc.

12. Discuss the sharing of personally owned teaching materials such as reference books, enrichment materials, and games.

13. Agree on one set of standards for grades, written evaluations, conferences, etc.

14. Make a list of mutually acceptable standards for portfolio assessments, if appropriate. Agree on an organized system by which to house and evaluate them.

15. Work out a system to maximize everyone's teaching time. For example, while one team member is doing an opening activity such as a "sponge" (see pages 281–283), another team member takes attendance, checks student make-up work, etc.

16. Plan team meeting times and stick to them. On occasion, hold a team meeting at a team member's home, or meet your team members at a restaurant to discuss something other than school.

17. Know your team members' birthdays and plan something special.

18. "He or she doesn't know what the other teachers are doing," is a frequent complaint about teaching teams made by parents, students, and other teachers; therefore, make it a point to know well what your team members are doing.

19. All team members need to take an equal and active part in Back-to-School Night or Parent Night (pages 103–105). What you say and model to parents, and the way in which you present it as a team, leaves a lasting impression.

20. Honestly, openly, and tactfully share concerns and problems with your teammates. If something is bothering you concerning another team member, find an appropriate time and way to discuss it directly with him or her. Do not let problems build up or continue for an inappropriate length of time.

21. Depending on your students' grade level, institute a system that allows parents to see their child's work on a regular basis. Consider using weekly student take-home packets (see pages 185–190).

22. Make it a point to have one parent/student phone log (see pages 191–193) in which each call by a team member to a student or parent is recorded. This will prevent duplicate phone calls from being made.

23. Be certain to have details well organized for parent-teacher conferences. For a checklist, refer to the section on parent-teacher conferences (pages 211–214).

24. Adopt procedural rules that make life easier for students who regularly work with many teachers, such as:

    ◆ heading papers the same (for example, placing the name, assignment, date, etc., in the same position on all papers)

    ◆ placing student signatures (peer grading) uniformly on each paper

    ◆ using the same grading scale and format for written evaluations

    ◆ receiving directions for assignments, group activities, projects, etc.

    ◆ logistics of handing in papers, obtaining make-up papers, etc.

    ◆ Policy for make-up or rewritten papers and their grades

25. Coordinate the ordering and use of audio-visual materials.

26. When necessary, request a full day's professional leave for a team meeting (one every semester, every 15–18 weeks, etc.). So much can be accomplished with no interruptions for an entire day! Plan your objectives carefully and submit them in writing to the principal or supervising administrator. Share your meeting's outcomes with the same person.

27. Never undermine a team member in front of students or parents. If you are experiencing significant problems with a particular person(s), talk to the team member(s) involved or to your administrator or principal.

Complete this checklist with some of your own ideas.

28. _____

_____

29. _____

_____

30. _____

_____

31. _____

_____

32. _____

_____

33. _____

_____

34. _____

_____

35. _____

_____

36. _____

_____

BACK-TO-SCHOOL NIGHT PREPARATION

Back-to-School Night provides an opportunity for you to briefly talk to parents about the curriculum, your background, expectations, teaching philosophy, classroom rules, and teaching materials.

Be prepared! Create a great first impression by being relaxed enough to be yourself. If you are well organized, you will feel more comfortable and your presentation will be more successful. The list on the following pages provides suggestions for making your back-to-school night presentation as thorough, dynamic, and informative as possible. Space has been left at the bottom of each section to allow you to add your own great ideas to the list.

BACK-TO-SCHOOL NIGHT

HANDOUTS

(These are important for parents to refer to after the presentation. They clarify and remind for those who choose not to take notes.)

◆ Write a brief summary or outline of the course content and include a general timeline if possible. Use a graphic organizer (see pages 235–247) for simplicity and a professional look.

◆ Summarize the following information on a one- to two-page handout:
  • classroom rules
  • grading procedures
  • expectations for late assignments
  • procedure for absences and getting assignments
  • your expectations for homework
  • your room number, phone number, and the times you are available to conference with students and parents
  • dates on which parents can expect to receive a monthly newsletter (see pages 178–184)
  • stress that this packet must be signed by themselves and their student and returned by a specific date (see pages 179–180).

◆ _____
  _____

◆ _____
  _____

◆ _____
  _____

THE PRESENTATION

◆ Use overhead transparencies whenever possible.
  • Overhead transparencies enable viewers to retain a great deal of information.
  • They reach diverse learning styles.
  • They keep you organized so that you will be less likely to omit information during your presentation.

◆ Write a brief outline of your presentation, and keep it handy.

◆ Begin with a quote, short anecdote, etc., to break the ice.

◆ Introduce yourself and give a brief description of your background. Include information you feel comfortable sharing related to:
  • education
  • previous teaching experiences, grade levels and courses taught, schools at which you taught, etc.
  • personal family background (married, children and their ages, etc.)
  • hobbies

◆ On a chalkboard or dry-erase board write how parents can contact you. Point to this information during the presentation to draw their attention to it. Also mention that the following information is included on your handout:
  • your name
  • office hours and office phone number
  • school phone number and extension

◆ Encourage general questions and tell parents to contact you at a later time regarding specific questions about their students.

DISTRIBUTE HANDOUTS

◆ Hold up and briefly discuss any texts or other materials used for the course.

◆ Clearly and briefly state your basic philosophy of teaching and learning and your expectations of students.

◆ Give a few concrete examples of how parents can help at home.

◆ Tell parents to watch for periodic "how to learn" sheets (see pages 194–210) that will accompany some homework assignments.

◆ Call attention to your classroom rules, discipline procedures, performance expectations, grading procedure, and when to return signed handouts.

◆ Point out student grade sheets, which allow each student to keep a record of his or her grades.

◆ Point out the potpourri table (see page 146) on which additional handouts are available for students at all times.

◆ Point out important bulletin boards, assignment calendars, the daily log binder, and your paper-return system (see page 137), which allows students access to their own make-up assignments.

◆ Summarize main points if necessary.

◆ Leave time for questions.

◆ _____
_____

◆ _____
_____

◆ _____
_____

◆ _____
_____

TEACHER EVALUATION

Being evaluated is stressful for almost everybody. When you care about your work, how others perceive the job you do matters a great deal. Unfortunately, negative comments are often remembered with more clarity and force than are positive comments. For that reason, an evaluation is not an easy process. However, evaluations serve a legitimate purpose, and those from your students are perhaps the most meaningful.

The information on the following pages provides suggestions for creating your own evaluations. The form on pages 108 and 109 is ready to be reproduced and used as an evaluative tool in your classroom.

Remember, the majority of students are generally quite honest and fair when evaluating their teachers, and some of the best ideas for improving teaching skills, content, projects, activities, assignments, and policies come from students.

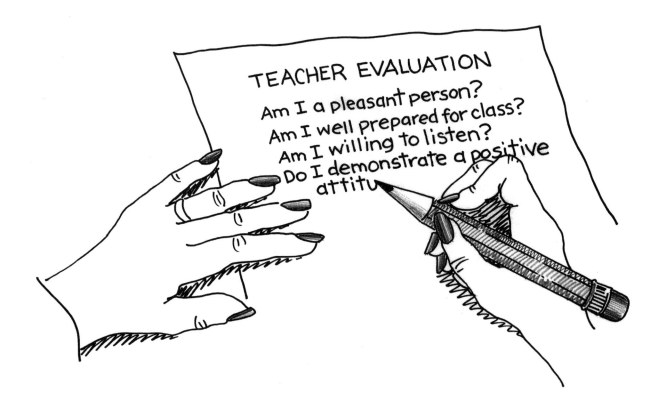

Teaching for Learning Success, Rev. Ed.

TEACHER EVALUATION

WHAT

A teacher evaluation is an assessment completed by students and administered at the end of the course.

WHY

Administer teacher evaluations to:

- ◆ provide feedback about your strengths as a teacher

- ◆ indicate areas that need improvement

- ◆ receive new ideas to incorporate into your curriculum the next time you teach this course

- ◆ provide feedback about activities, ideas, systems, etc., you should either continue with or change before using again

HOW

Write a brief introductory paragraph that includes the following:

- ◆ the purpose of the evaluation

- ◆ simple directions

- ◆ names are optional

- ◆ the evaluation will not affect anyone's grade

- ◆ only sincere and honest comments are welcome

Decide on the rating system you prefer:

- ◆ points

- ◆ letter grades

- ◆ check marks in appropriate columns

Provide space for comments.

Ask direct questions that require brief responses.

Give adequate class time for completion during the last week of the course. (This activity works best if it is not issued on the last day of class.)

Tally results using an extra copy of the evaluation.

Read through comments and jot down ideas and notes.

Keep an open, objective mind.

TEACHER EVALUATION

Teacher _____ Class _____ Period _____ Date _____

Directions: Please answer the following questions by placing a check in the appropriate columns on the right-hand side of the page. Your honest and sincere responses are appreciated. I will use this evaluation to improve my teaching skills and this course in general. Writing your name on this evaluation is optional. This will not affect your grade in any way.	Usually	Sometimes	Hardly Ever
Am I a pleasant person?			
Am I well prepared for class?			
Am I willing to help students when they need it?			
Do I demonstrate that I care about your learning?			
Do you learn from me?			
Do I demonstrate knowledge of this subject?			
Are my expectations for your achievements realistic and fair?			
Do I show enthusiasm toward students and teaching?			
Can you count on me to follow through when you need it?			
Do I use a sense of humor appropriately?			
Is the work I expect students to do realistic and meaningful?			
Do I give good directions?			
Am I fair to all students?			
Is the classroom organized so that you can find things when you need them?			
Do I listen to students?			
Do I demonstrate respect for students?			
Are my plans for each class thorough and understandable?			
Are my daily assignments appropriate?			
Am I optimistic and do I think of students in a positive way?			
Do I use a variety of approaches to teach to all students?			
Am I willing to change my plans and ideas when possible?			
Am I relaxed and easygoing in class?			

©2004 by Incentive Publications, Inc., Nashville, TN *Teaching for Learning Success, Rev. Ed.*
Acknowledgement of credit is made to Krista Brakhage for the above material.

	Usually	Sometimes	Hardly Ever
Do you have fun learning in my class most of the time?			
Do I encourage you to take responsibility for your own learning?			
Is my classroom interesting, colorful, and a place you like to be?			
Do I begin class with stimulating activities?			
Do you think I dress appropriately for a teacher?			
Do I give fair tests?			

What would you change? _____

_____

_____

What did you like about me or the class? What would you keep? _____

_____

_____

What was your favorite topic, project, assignment, activity, etc.? _____

_____

_____

_____

Comments: _____

_____

_____

_____

©2004 by Incentive Publications, Inc., Nashville, TN
Acknowledgement of credit is made to Krista Brakhage for the above material.

34 QUICK TIPS:
Why Didn't I Think of That?

1. Use clear, non-shiny contact paper to cover any items you wish to write on with transparency pens and reuse next year.

2. Secure schedules and other reference sheets to the top of any surface by covering them with clear contact paper that has been cut a little larger than the pages themselves. This holds the papers in place and protects them at the same time.

3. Post on your classroom walls several daily schedules large enough to be read from a distance.

4. Always keep sets of handouts suitable for impromptu Switch games (see pages 287–288). Label and place in file cabinet.

5. Always test any equipment before class begins.

6. Call your local newspaper and ask for end rolls of newsprint for your classroom. These rolls contain yards of continuous blank paper suitable for many uses: murals, group projects, bulletin boards, etc.

7. Reuse file folders by folding them inside-out or applying new adhesive labels.

8. Make two-sided photocopies when possible to save paper.

9. Organize papers and sets of handouts in a large cardboard shoe divider. Cut small strips of 3" x 5" index cards for labels and attach one to each compartment.

10. When stacking sets of papers, insert one sheet of colored paper between each set; alternate positions of paper clips along the tops of the sets so that the stack will be relatively flat.

11. Follow these steps when collating handouts into packets or booklets if the copy machine does not do it:
    - Arrange the stacks of papers on a countertop, table, or student desks pushed together.
    - Place rubber finger pads on your thumb and index finger.
    - Picking up the last page first, walk toward the first page, pausing just long enough to add the appropriate page to the top of your pile.
    - Hold the pile of papers in your left hand, and add the papers to your stack with your right hand (if this feels uncomfortable, switch hands).
    - After completing one packet, crisscross each additional packet, and staple all packets at one time.

    Remember, it is easier and quicker to add papers to the top of a stack than to the bottom.

12. Make handouts for each class two weeks in advance. (It takes about two weeks to repair a broken copy machine.)

13. Maintain a separate file folder that contains a copy of every handout you give to your classes. This "artifacts" file provides quicker access to your handouts than does keeping them in your content files.

14. Always make 2–3 extra copies of every handout for:
    ◆ replacements when the copy machine "goofed" on a copy or two
    ◆ your artifacts file (see #13 above)
    ◆ for the "extra handouts" box on the potpourri table (see page 146)

15. Always keep valuables (such as your purse or wallet) in a locked desk or file drawer.

16. For quick location of materials, label file drawers by using colored paper to match your class calendars and paper return folders.

17. It is easier to correct papers in class if you use as your answer sheet a copy of the students' test with the answers included. Many times, a simple list of answers is insufficient to allow you to successfully comprehend a question that a student may ask about the test.

18. Clip answer sheets to the master copy and file them.

19. Keep answer sheets safe by placing them inside plastic page-covers or covering them with contact paper. Organize them in labeled binders.

20. Always keep old tests and answer keys filed with your unit plans for future reference and revision.

21. Begin a file of useful information to include in monthly parent newsletters or use at parent-teacher conferences or a Back-to-School Night. Parents will appreciate articles on teaching and child development, book reviews, quotes from professional journals that apply to students' experiences, convention handouts, etc. Be mindful of copyrights.

22. Always make a copy of anything you consider important (individual letters or notes sent home, principal communiques, etc.) and file them for future reference.

23. Write a brief agenda of each day's class on the chalkboard, dry-erase board, or transparency each morning. This takes only a few minutes and prevents you from having to answer, "What are we doing today?" over and over again. It can also help to keep you on track.

24. If you change classrooms during the day, take with you:
    ◆ seating chart (see pages 141–142)
    ◆ attendance slips
    ◆ discipline referral slips
    ◆ hall passes
    ◆ textbook checkout list (see pages 147–148)
    ◆ appropriate handouts
    ◆ lesson plans

- teacher's edition of text
- special equipment
- "sign up" notebook for your discipline system (see pages 124–129)
- appropriate personal items

25. Set aside time to "catch up" on lesson plans, reports, and papers to be graded. Keeping up with these chores is the greatest mental health booster possible for professional teachers.

26. Tardies? Try giving a short quiz covering the previous day's material as soon as class starts. These quizzes cannot be made up by anyone who misses them because of lateness. A short quiz makes a great review for those students who are present, and the underlying message of the quiz is quickly understood by the tardy students.

27. Have students return papers, distribute handouts, and complete other classroom tasks. It saves you time and involves them in classroom activities. Be sure to check building and district policies regarding students seeing other student grades.

28. Begin your classroom preparation two days before other faculty members return to school in the fall. You will find that you can accomplish a great deal when away from the interruptions of curious colleagues. The copy machine will be available, as well.

29. Change your seating chart every nine weeks. Students appreciate being given the opportunity to sit next to different people throughout the school year.

30. Attending a convention provides a mental lift and reignites your enthusiasm for teaching. Go when you can.
    - If the convention offers numerous "break-out sessions," carefully read the program brochure and select your sessions before you attend.
    - Go with a friend if possible; it is more fun, and two can attend more sessions than one. Pick up an extra handout to share.
    - Arrive early at the sessions; sit in the front of the room to have a better view and to receive all handouts (often, handouts never make it to the back of the room).
    - Allow plenty of time to visit the trade book section.

31. Try to avoid giving tests on Fridays.

32. During the first week of class, inform students that you will usually use some type of signal when you want their attention. It can be a raised hand or quietly standing at the front of the room. Clue them in on your body language.

33. Keep a list of important names and addresses handy: include teachers' state associations, community resources, volunteer parents you use frequently, etc. Use 3" x 5" card files, a rolodex, or an address book.

34. You never get a second chance to make a good first impression. What image of yourself would you like to present to others? If you choose to dress like your students, they will treat you like a peer. If you choose to dress like a professional, they will realize you mean business.

ORGANIZING YOUR CLASSROOM

✍ *Indicates ready-to-use forms or handouts*

ORGANIZING YOUR CLASSROOM:

An Overview

Well-organized teachers who manage their classrooms effectively leave no time for discipline problems. Learning is the focus of these teachers' classrooms, and their students know it. Students function better when clearly defined rules have been established and in physical surroundings that are designed for efficiency and a pleasant learning environment. The practical ideas, checklists, and forms in this chapter include strategies and tips to help you organize your classroom for student success.

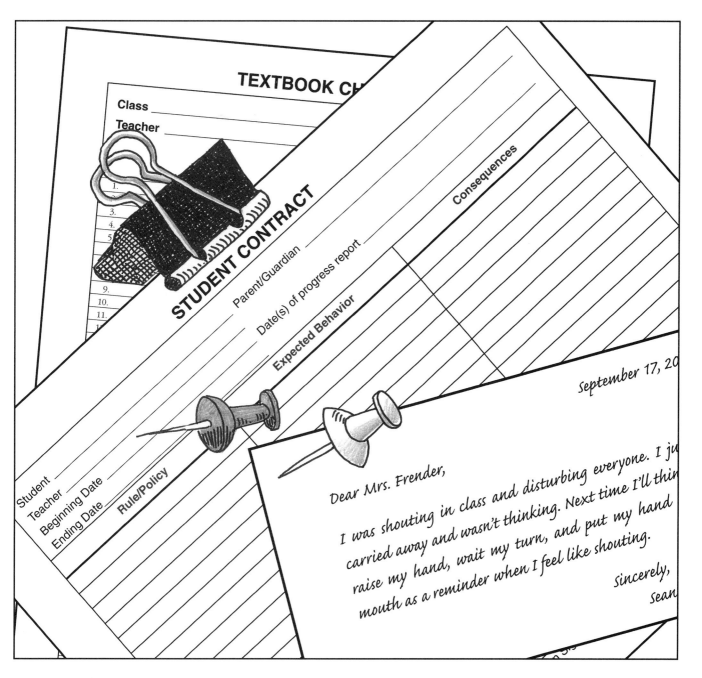

CREATING A GOOD LEARNING ENVIRONMENT

How you choose to arrange the physical components of your classroom sets the tone for your learning environment. Create a positive learning environment by making your classroom personable, inviting, and interesting—a place in which you and your students will enjoy spending a great deal of time. Consider the following suggestions before designing your room.

SAFETY

Emergency Exits
- Do not block emergency exits.
- Provide a clear traffic pattern between desks or tables and around the perimeter of the room.

Electrical Cords
- Keep electrical cords out of traffic patterns.
- Do not overload electrical circuits.

Storage
- Safely store equipment, books, and supplies so that they are secure from student access, if needed.
- Arrange items so that they will not fall or move easily.

Handicap Accessibility
- Widen aisles, provide ramps, or make any necessary adjustments.

Ventilation
- Make sure there is adequate ventilation for the entire room.
- Maintain heating and cooling systems for the classroom.

VISIBILITY

Chalkboards/Dry-erase Boards/Screens/Monitors
- Be aware of how light reflects on these objects at different times throughout the day.
- Make sure that all students can see them, even at the back of the room.
- Make sure that they are easily accessible to both you and your students.

Windows
- Be aware of how and when light shines through your room's windows—bright sunlight can be very distracting!

Teaching for Learning Success, Rev. Ed.

- Make sure that the blinds or shades work properly.
- Do not face student desks directly in front of a window.
- Position the teacher's desk so that sunlight from the windows does not block your view of the students or any part of the classroom.
- Be aware that a view of the outside can be a major source of distraction for students—arrange seating so that the students' attention will be directed to the front of the classroom.

Overhead Projector
- Before class begins, experiment to gauge how well the information on a transparency can be seen by the entire class.
- Know which bank of lights interferes with the visibility of the overhead.

Computer Equipment
- Consider how light reflects on the monitor.
- Be aware of the traffic pattern around each computer station.
- Take into consideration access to necessary electrical hook-ups and how many computer stations can run off certain circuits.
- Know the types of resources students will need when working at the computer station(s), and provide easy access to these items by placing an extra table or set of bookshelves adjacent to the computers.

Lectern or Podium
- Before setting up a lectern or podium, decide how much use it will receive.

Student Desks
- Consider the degree of student interaction that is appropriate for your teaching style and arrange desks accordingly (in single rows, double rows, clusters, half of the room facing the other half, etc.).
- Consider comfortable traffic patterns when planning the arrangement of student desks.
- Know that students seated near chalkboards, bookshelves, supplies, and equipment will be tempted to touch or mark on these items.
- Have the desktops cleaned regularly.

Student Tables
- Do not overcrowd the number of students per table.
- Supply students with a place to store belongings while in your classroom, as most tables have no storage space for extra books, notebooks, etc. Check building policy regarding backpacks.
- Be aware that some students will need to move their chairs to complete certain activities.
- Consider the amount of student interaction that is probable.
- Provide for a traffic pattern.
- Have the tabletops cleaned regularly.

USABILITY

Teacher's Desk

- ◆ Be considerate when using this space. Avoid making the teacher's desk the center of attention—place it in a corner or to the side of the room.
- ◆ Consider making the teacher's desk accessible to students from one side only to ensure that students can approach the desk only one at a time.
- ◆ Place the teacher's desk within reach of filing cabinets, bookshelves, or other materials you need.
- ◆ Carefully consider items placed on the desktop for safety, clutter, and loss factors.

Extra Tables for Study Purposes

- ◆ If you have extra classroom space and your teaching style and class activities utilize small group work occasionally, set up a table and extra chairs in a quiet corner of the room.
- ◆ Carefully place computer work stations and consider distractibility, safety, useability, etc.

Extra Table for Papers, etc. (see page 146)

- ◆ Consider setting up a small table on which to place extra credit work, handouts continually used by students, classroom materials, etc.
- ◆ Place this table in an area that is easily accessible to students.
- ◆ Keep it organized, clean, and as uncluttered as possible.

Wastebaskets

- ◆ Place at least two wastebaskets in the classroom—one near your desk and the other accessible to students, but removed from traffic patterns.

PHYSICAL ATMOSPHERE

Color

- ◆ Using bright colors whenever possible makes your learning environment interesting and inviting.
- ◆ Use color when you mount posters, display student papers, assemble bulletin boards, make transparencies, hang items from the ceiling, label filing cabinet drawers, make banners, etc.
- ◆ Consider using fabric as an alternative to colored paper.

Posters, Banners, and Signs

- ◆ Hang student-oriented posters, banners, signs, etc.
- ◆ Change them regularly.
- ◆ Hang posters that reveal a sense of humor and lightheartedness.

Plants

- ◆ Consider adding some plants to your classroom—they create a warm atmosphere.
- ◆ Plants need varying amounts of light and water and should be placed away from direct contact with students or heat sources.
- ◆ During school vacations of more than a week, group plants together, provide a watering can, and write a note with care instructions to the janitor. Talk to him or her before leaving.
- ◆ Purchase easy-care, hardy plants—know how much light enters your room before deciding on a variety.

Boxes, Paper Organizers, etc.

- ◆ Consider a colorful "Student Comments" box for student input; provide slips of paper by cutting apart and reusing old handouts.
- ◆ Place colorful plastic boxes or paper organizers on the potpourri table, the teacher's desk, etc.

Additional Furniture

- ◆ Place bean bag chairs in a reading corner.
- ◆ Use freestanding bookshelves anchored to the wall to provide room dividers.
- ◆ Consider installing carpeting in some areas. (Visit carpet shops, acquire large samples, and sew them together or use carpet tape on the back side.)

MENTAL ATMOSPHERE

Sense of Humor

- ◆ Whenever possible, use a sense of humor to handle a situation—students will still understand your message, but appreciate it more.
- ◆ Strive to be appropriately entertaining—demonstrate active (not passive) learning by sharing genuine excitement with your students.

Be Positive

- ◆ When writing rules, comments on papers, etc., stress the positive aspects more heavily than the negative ones; insist on an atmosphere of constructive criticism.
- ◆ Choose positive words when responding orally to student comments. If it is not the answer or comment you were expecting, say, "That's an interesting answer. What's your thinking behind it?" (See page 34.)
- ◆ Be aware of how students perceive you; your intentions and your students' perceptions may be completely different.

CREATING A GOOD LEARNING ENVIRONMENT

Be Fair
- Students respect fairness.
- Unless it is fair to everyone, don't say it, don't do it, and don't write it.
- Be consistent: mean what you say, and say what you mean.
- When dealing with a disciplinary matter, talk with a student in the hall instead of in the classroom in front of the student's peers—some students thrive on negative attention in front of their peers, but demonstrate different behavior when alone.

Be Honest
- Create an atmosphere of trust by always being honest with your students.
- Students are more willing to try but risk making mistakes if they know that their teacher does the same.

Show Your Personal Side
- Research reveals that students learn more from teachers they like.
- Share a few of your own experiences as they relate to the subject being covered—be personable.
- Be the type of teacher from whom you would like to learn.

Be Open
- Be open to observing causes for disruption or unacceptable behavior before just jumping in to handle it.
- Be open to change.
- Be open to new ideas.
- Be open to student responses—try to figure out a student's motivation when answering a question before judging it incorrect.

Teaching for Learning Success, Rev. Ed.

DISCIPLINE SUGGESTIONS
For a "Win-Win" Atmosphere

Students do not learn without some form of discipline; however, you do not have to run your classroom with an "iron fist." The best way to prevent discipline problems is to be organized in classroom management and consistent in reinforcing classroom rules. The following list of facts, suggestions, and helpful hints will assist you in creating a balanced and equitable discipline plan that stresses maximum teaching and minimum policing time. Examine each element carefully and compile the best discipline system for your teaching style. (Refer to "Sign-up": A Discipline System that Works!, pages 124–129.)

1. Demonstrate respect for all students. Command respect from all students.

2. All students like and function best with boundaries, routines, and order.

3. Make all rules and policies straightforward; leave no room for interpretation.

4. Avoid making rules or policies that are difficult to enforce.

5. The fewer essential rules the better. Insist on no more than five essential classroom rules.

6. As soon as the school year begins, discuss all classroom rules with students so that everyone thoroughly understands your policies.

7. Hold high but reasonable expectations. Your students usually live up to them.

8. Be a good role model.

9. Review your expectations for student behavior with substitute teachers.

10. Establish control and a sense of presence from the very first day. Make it a habit to walk around the classroom.

11. Let students know that everyone is responsible for maintaining a good learning atmosphere. Students (not you) will be held responsible for their behavior. Your role is to enforce policies and rules should students decide to break them.

12. Make students believe that you have eyes in the back of your head.

13. Use a sense of humor as your first response to discipline problems whenever appropriate. Students understand your message and don't feel "put down." They remember the lesson longer, too.

DISCIPLINE SUGGESTIONS

14. Whenever possible, use nonverbal signals to convey messages to students. Standing near or sitting on a disruptive student's desk quickly conveys your message, and you don't have to "miss a beat" in your teaching!

15. Never give a student an audience for negative behavior. If you cannot immediately diffuse a disruptive situation, remove the student causing the problem from the classroom setting, and talk with that student in the hall or an adjacent classroom.

16. Do not engage in a shouting match with a student. Give yourself time to calm down and formulate a response instead of reacting angrily to a disruptive student. Notify the student of any inappropriate behavior, and tell him or her that you will discuss his or her behavior at the end of class. The louder and more aggressive the student becomes, the quieter and calmer you become. It works!

17. Preventative medicine is the best cure. Be observant. If you see early signs of disruptive behavior, diffuse it before it gets started. Restate your expectations for student behavior along with the directions for the activity or assignment in which you are engaged. Refocus the student's attention on the task.

18. Control your classroom learning environment by your love of teaching and students, not by intimidation and fear.

19. Attack behavior, not people.

20. Don't be afraid of appearing human to your students. Tell students when you are mad or that your feelings have been hurt. They need to view you as a "real" person.

21. Always look for the cause of a student's negative behavior. It may not be directly linked to the immediate problem or have anything to do with the student's school environment.

22. Handle your own classroom's discipline problems whenever possible. Students will have more respect for you if you do. Only if student behavior is unsafe or completely disruptive to the entire class, and after you have tried all possible intervening steps, should you send the student to the administrative office.

23. Keep in mind that being sent in the hallway for the duration of the class is most often viewed by students as a reward, not a punishment. They most likely will disrupt other classes as well.

24. There is a saying that has been around a long time and which still applies to the classroom: "Be an active, not a reactive, teacher."

25. Inform your class that you know the games that students play (even if you don't!), and that you are not a player. If you do not expect any power struggles, there probably will not be any.

Teaching for Learning Success, Rev. Ed.

26. Tell your class what pleases you and what displeases you—they will respond positively to your candor.

27. Try to "win over" the most disruptive student early in the course or year. He or she can become an important ally as other students often take their cues from him or her.

28. Do not hold grudges against your students. Once a problem has been solved, forget about it. Try your best to start anew each day.

29. Always supply a written set of your rules and discipline procedures to your principal, vice principal, dean of students, counselors, and anyone else that might handle disciplinary matters.

30. Make it a point to keep your students so busy and engaged in learning that there is no time for negative behavior.

31. Carefully observe your students for unspoken messages that might develop into negative behavior.

32. Maintain, but don't flaunt, your control of the classroom.

33. Use only meaningful and sincere praise. Students know if you are being honest.

34. As the teacher, you are in charge of the "success department." Be sure that everyone has an equal and frequent opportunity to visit there.

35. Students learn and thrive from encouragement, not discouragement.

36. Let students know that you think they are intelligent and can make good decisions.

37. Tell your students, "I have faith in you! You can do it!"

38. If you dress for authority, you will be more likely to receive it.

"SIGN-UP":
—————— A Discipline System that Works! ——————

WHAT

The discipline system outlined on the following pages has proven successful for students of all grade levels; parents, teachers, and administrators also agree on its effectiveness. It is a good idea to read through the entire set of instructions in order to understand the program as a whole. Although the directions and recommendations appear lengthy, this disciplinary system is actually simple to implement and enforce.

One reason the "sign-up" system works so well is that students view it as fair. It is also successful because it places the responsibility for student behavior on the student (not the teacher); the student is made to document and sign his or her name to all disruptive behavior. Parents are also kept informed of the entire process, and the student sees a demonstrated effort by teacher, principal, and parents, who are all working together in the student's best interest.

The "sign-up" system provides for the best:

♦ active student participation in correcting negative behavior

♦ home/school communication

♦ documentation providing "incriminating evidence" against students

♦ approach to take with students who search for ways to "beat the system"

WHY

♦ This system makes the student (not the teacher!) responsible for his or her own actions.

♦ It sends a strong message to the student that parents and teacher are working together for the benefit of his or her learning.

♦ This system does not take up a great amount of your planning period or after-school time.

♦ It is a simple system to administer and records are easily maintained.

♦ Everything is documented, dated, and signed by the student.

♦ It improves school/home communication and focuses on the student's behavior.

♦ The system's rules are easily understood by everyone.

♦ The warning system gives the student ample time to change his or her negative behavior before being punished.

Teaching for Learning Success, Rev. Ed.

◆ This system affords dignity to all students with no lecturing about their behavior.

◆ Students find the system's realistic and concrete rules to be fair for all.

MATERIALS

◆ spiral notebook with ruled paper

◆ pen or pencil attached to the spiral

◆ felt-tip pen for writing on posterboard or computer printout of classroom rules

◆ one labeled file folder per class

◆ posterboard for permanent display of classroom rules and discipline system

◆ part of a bulletin board or wall space on which to place the posterboard or printout

TO DO BEFORE CLASSES BEGIN

1. Make a computer printout, or, using a felt-tip pen, write the heading "Room Rules" at the top of a large piece of posterboard. Directly under the heading list the rules that:

◆ you feel comfortable reinforcing on a continual basis

◆ provide a good teaching and learning atmosphere

◆ provide safety for all students

◆ are consistent with your school's and district's rules

◆ can be fairly administered to all students

◆ are concrete, not abstract

◆ are simply and generically written, but specifically understood

Remember: Keep them simple and few.

For example, you might want to post these fundamental rules:

Room Rules

◆ Come to class prepared and on time.

◆ Respect everyone's right to learn.

◆ Respect school and personal property.

◆ No food, gum, hats, toys, etc.

◆ Do not throw anything at any time.

2. Write the heading "Consequences" below the rules. Directly under the heading, write the discipline system's procedures.

Consequences

Step One: a verbal or nonverbal warning

Step Two: "sign-up"

Step Three: "sign-up" and a letter

Step Four: three letters = student-parent-teacher conference

Step Five: four letters = student-parent-teacher-principal conference

3. Write the date at the top of a page in a lined, spiral notebook, divide the page into the appropriate number of classes for that day, and label each accordingly. To save time and effort, organize the entire notebook all at once for a month at a time.

4. Attach a pen or a pencil to the spiral notebook with a string.

5. Place the notebook in an accessible part of the classroom, such as the chalkboard or dry-erase board tray or on the potpourri table (see page 146).

TO DO WHEN CLASSES BEGIN

1. Make clear your expectations for student behavior.

2. Use specific examples to clarify your position on each rule. All rules and consequences should be unambiguous—no shades of gray.

3. State that each student (not you) is responsible for his or her own actions.

4. Inform students that you will be working closely with their parents throughout the year.

5. State your position as a teacher who is responsible for maintaining a good learning atmosphere and who will enforce rules fairly for everyone's benefit; however, let your students know that you do not intend to assume a policeperson's role. Your major role is to teach.

6. Let students view the sign-up notebook, and show them where it will be placed in the classroom.

THE "SIGN-UP" SYSTEM

(Each day students start with a "clean slate". Sign-ups are not carried over from day to day.)

STEP ONE: Verbal/Nonverbal Warning

1. Give specific examples of the types of verbal warnings you will give; you might say: "Sean, this is a warning."

2. Give specific examples of the types of nonverbal warnings you will give; you might use a variety of facial expressions (a frown, a stare, etc.) or specific body language (sitting on a student's desk, standing near a student's desk, etc.).

3. After issuing the warning, ask the student if he or she knows why the warning is being issued. Wait for the student's reply. A simple "yes" or "no" answer is sufficient.

STEP TWO: Sign-up

1. If the student continues to break the same rule or breaks a different one after a warning has been given, give the student a second warning.

2. Upon being issued a second warning, the student is required to legibly write his or her first and last name in the appropriate place in the sign-up notebook.

3. You will then ask the student if he or she knows why he or she is being asked to sign the notebook. A simple "yes" or "no" response is expected.

STEP THREE: Sign-up and Letter

1. Enforce step three if the student continues to break the same rule or breaks a different rule and has signed the notebook one time.

2. Ask the student to sign the notebook again.

3. In addition to signing the notebook a second time, require the student to write a letter during his or her free time. The letter should contain three statements:
   ◆ what the student did to break the rule
   ◆ why the student broke the rule
   ◆ what the student will do in the future to correct this behavior (this statement must be concrete and realistic)

The letter should contain no mechanical errors, should be written in correct letter format and dated, and will be rewritten, if necessary, until considered acceptable by the teacher.

Sample student letter:

September 17, 2004

Dear Mrs. Frender,

I was shouting in class and disturbing everyone. I just got carried away and wasn't thinking. Next time I'll think first, raise my hand, wait my turn, and put my hand over my mouth as a reminder when I feel like shouting.

Sincerely,

Sean Johnston

4. The letter will be placed in the file folder for that class; all future letters pertaining to that student will be stapled together.

5. If a student is required to write three letters within one quarter or grading period, the following will happen:

   ◆ A copy of all of the letters will be sent home with the student for parental signature (the teacher keeps all originals).

   ◆ The teacher will call home to arrange a student-parent-teacher conference (see Step Four below).

Suggestion: When giving the letters to the student to take home, remind the student you will be calling home and that it would be to the student's advantage to discuss the letters with his or her parent(s) before they receive your call.

STEP FOUR: Student-Parent-Teacher Conference

1. Introduce yourself, if necessary, to your student's parent(s).

2. Seat the student between the parent(s) and yourself at a table.

3. Give the original letters to the student (if he or she did not bring the copies to the conference).

4. State the purpose of the meeting. You might say: "Sean, the purpose of this conference is to help you change your behavior so that you can learn more in class and not distract other students or disturb the learning atmosphere. Please explain these letters to your parents and me."

5. As the teacher, play only a minor part in the conference, and let the student and parent(s) do the majority of the talking. Clarify certain points when necessary, keep the meeting focused on the purpose, and mention the student's positive behavior when appropriate.

6. Take notes as needed.

7. At the conclusion of the conference:

   ◆ Summarize realistic, specific actions the student can demonstrate in class.

   ◆ Make sure that the student clearly understands the rules and verbally summarizes his or her "plan of attack" to correct the negative behavior.

   ◆ Make sure that the student understands that he or she is directly responsible for his or her actions and that you expect to see an immediate change in behavior.

   ◆ Make sure that both student and parent(s) understand the next step to be taken if this or other negative behavior continues (see Step Five below).

8. Summarize in writing the actions leading to this conference and the specific actions to be taken to change the student's behavior.

9. Date, sign, and have the student and parent(s) sign this summary. Make a copy of the summary for the parent(s), and file it, along with the original letters, in a file folder for future reference.

STEP FIVE: Student-Parent-Teacher-Principal Conference

1. Execute Step Five after a student has accumulated a total of four letters and has participated in a parent-teacher conference.

2. Before the meeting, review with your principal the steps you have taken thus far, and share with him or her the student letters and signed summary of the initial conference.

3. Include the principal in a second student-parent-teacher conference (see Step Four above).

4. During the second conference, present all previous letters and the written summary of the initial conference.

5. Require the student to explain the letters to everyone.

6. Again, summarize in writing the actions to be taken and have everyone involved sign the summary.

7. Make a copy of the summary for the student's parent(s) and the principal.

8. Clip all papers together and file them in the appropriate folder.

STUDENT CONTRACTS

Occasionally, a student in your class will not respond to your usual system of discipline. Try using a contract with this student.

In the contract, identify your classroom rules, the student's negative behavior, and the consequences of his or her actions. If a time limit for rectifying the behavior is appropriate, set one. Discuss your recommendations with the student, his or her parent(s), the counselor, and school administrator(s). It is best if everyone involved can attend a conference in order to clearly understand the contract.

Ask the student to read through the contract and relate what it says in his or her own words. Ask for any input the student may have, whether the student has any questions, and if the parents have any input or questions. Ask others involved in the conference for input and questions.

Make necessary arrangements to keep others informed regarding the student's progress.

The most important attributes of a student contract are:

- a clear understanding of the rules, expected behavior, and consequences of disruptive behavior

- a timely follow-through by all those involved

A sample student contract is provided on the following page.

STUDENT CONTRACT

Student _____

Teacher _____

Beginning Date _____

Ending Date _____

Parent/Guardian _____

Date(s) of progress report _____

Rule/Policy	Expected Behavior	Consequences

Comments: _____

I have read and discussed this contract. I understand the rules, the behavior expected, and the consequences.

_____ _____
Student Signature   Parent/Guardian Signature   Teacher Signature

KEEPING TRACK OF ASSIGNMENTS

Keeping track of assignments can be a difficult, frustrating, and time-consuming task, but it does not have to be! The three-part tracking system outlined on the following pages will allow you and your students to maintain an accurate and organized up-to-date record of upcoming, missed, and overdue assignments.

What makes this system so successful?

◆ It places on the student the responsibility of locating and completing missed assignments.

◆ All parts of this system are available to students all of the time.

◆ It is easy to maintain.

◆ It provides a comprehensive system that parents readily understand and appreciate.

◆ It is easily understood by substitute teachers and operates smoothly even if you are not in class.

This system is composed of three elements:

◆ large calendars posted on a bulletin board or wall in the classroom and individual student monthly calendar handouts

◆ student paper-return folders

◆ three-ring binder

HELPFUL HINTS

This system works most effectively when all of its elements are placed together in the classroom. For example, the large calendars can be posted on a bulletin board, and the paper-return folders and three-ring binder can be placed on a table standing beneath or near the bulletin board.

Whenever possible, color-code everything having to do with one subject, class, or period using the same color. This will alleviate a great deal of student confusion and prevent simple recording errors. Make sure that the directions for your assignment tracking system are clearly marked and logged in the substitute folder.

Discuss the assignment tracking system with students during the first week of school. Always ask for questions, and be sure to stress the following:

◆ Students are responsible for keeping track of their make-up assignments.

◆ Students are responsible for checking all three parts of this system each time they return to class following an absence.

◆ Each student will be responsible for entering class activities and assignments in the daily log binder on a rotating weekly basis.

Teaching for Learning Success, Rev. Ed.

PART 1:
CALENDARS

Large Calendars

1. Purchase large (23" x 28") blank calendars. These are usually printed on posterboard and can be found at educational supply stores, office supply stores, or through office supply catalogs. Purchase one calendar for each class, period, or subject that you teach, and color-code them (by class, period, or subject) to coordinate with the other parts of this system.

2. Cover each calendar with clear dull-finish contact paper.

3. Post calendars in an easy-to-access, highly visible area of the classroom.

4. Label each calendar according to subject area, period, or class.

5. Keep black water-soluble transparency pens in the teacher's desk. These pens work well on the contact paper and wipe clean with a damp paper towel and dry paper towel.

6. Write each assignment and its due date on the calendar. As you write the assignment on the large calendar, students should be copying it onto their monthly calendar handouts. If you have already written the assignment during a previous class, point to it on the calendar as you discuss it, giving time to students to write it on their individual calendars.

7. Post long-term as well as short-term assignments. For long-term assignments, it is helpful to write a large "1/2" on the date the project should be half completed. Do the same for the dates on which the assignment should be one-fourth and three-fourths complete. Discuss three steps that should be completed at each benchmark date: for example "research finished," "note cards completed," etc.

KEEPING TRACK OF ASSIGNMENTS

Student Calendars

The blank calendar master form on the following page may be reproduced and distributed to each student on the first school day of each month. You may want to write in the dates of quizzes, tests, long-term assignments, special events, vacation days, etc., before reproducing the calendar. Make a transparency of the calendar for use on the overhead projector and write in the assignments as a guide for the students to follow. You may also want to use this calendar as a class syllabus.

Take a few minutes at the beginning of class on the first school day of each month to fill in the large calendar on the bulletin board. Students will copy the assignments and activities onto their individual calendars as you write them on the master calendar. As you continue to add assignments throughout the month, remind students to add them to their personal copies.

It is a good idea to keep several extra blank student calendars on the potpourri table (see page 146) so that students may replace lost calendars themselves.

MONTH: _____

Name _____ **Period** _____

Teacher _____ **Class** _____

Sunday	Monday	Tuesday	Wednesday	Thursday	Friday	Saturday

Notes:

	Assignment	Due Date	Estimated Time	Materials Needed	Done
THIS WEEK					
LATER					

WEEK OF _____

	MATERIAL TESTED	TEST DATE	TYPE OF TEST	SPECIAL NOTES
EXAMS				

PART 2:
PAPER-RETURN FOLDERS

1. Use a 9" x 12", colored and labeled file folder for each class, subject, or period.

2. Match this file folder with the large calendar of the same color.

3. Place these folders chronologically in a file sorter that allows files to sit upright.

4. Place all absent students' papers in the corresponding files when handing back papers.When taking attendance at the beginning of class, keep all handouts for that class period nearby so that you can write the names of absent students directly on the handouts and immediately place them in the correct paper-return file folder.

Helpful Hints

◆ Keep for yourself a labeled file folder for each class, period, or subject, and when distributing handouts drop an extra copy in the appropriate folder for your reference. This system is helpful if you need to quickly make a copy of a handout for any reason. It saves time that would be spent digging through your files.

◆ Keep a box or tray labeled "extra handouts" next to the paper-return folders. Place all extra handouts in the box for student use. A good paper-saving policy, as well as one which instills student responsibility, is to hold each student responsible for making his or her own copy of a lost handout.

PART 3:
DAILY LOG BINDER

1. Use a three-ring binder that has been divided into sections with colored tabs (one per class, subject, or period), several copies of the master form for daily log entries on page 140, and one copy of the daily log instructions on page 139.

2. Label the tabs for each class, subject, or period. Be sure to color-code each label according to the colors used on the calendars and paper-return folders.

3. Label the front and spine of the binder "Daily Log."

4. Assemble the book chronologically, and place several copies of the daily log in the front of each section.

5. Insert the instruction page in the front of the binder or adhere it to the inside cover.

6. On a chalkboard or a dry-erase board, write the name of one student per class or period who will be responsible for logging the daily entries that week. Change the name on a weekly basis.

7. Review the following procedure with your students.

    ◆ Each day for a week, the student whose name is listed on the board will pick up the binder at the beginning of class and return it to its place at the end of the class.

    ◆ The student records all of the week's assignments in the notebook.

    ◆ In addition to writing the title and due date of each assignment, every day the student is expected to write a brief summary of any activities that occurred during class. This allows absent students to know what occurred in class, even if no assignments were given.

    ◆ Each student should always fill in the date and his or her name so that absent students know who to contact with additional questions.

    ◆ Be sure to return the binder to the correct table at the end of class for the next class to use.

STUDENT DIRECTIONS FOR DAILY LOGS

You are responsible for writing a short summary of each class and recording all assignments in the daily log every day for a period of one week. Other students are depending on you to make this record complete so that they can get missed assignments and catch up on any class activities they missed while absent.

Always pick up this binder at the beginning of class, enter any important information and assignments in appropriate places, and return it at the end of class.

Follow these steps:

1. Find the tab that represents your class and open the folder to that page.

2. Write today's date in the "Date" column.

3. Write your first and last name in the "Name" column.

4. Write a short summary of today's activities and assignments. Use more than one space if necessary. Include the date the assignment is due.

5. At the end of class, return this binder to its proper place.

6. Repeat this each day for a period of one week.

EXAMPLE:

Date	Name	Assignments and Class Activities
9/9	Jennifer Martin	Discussion on short story formats; read pp. 34-47
		in text; answer quest. 1-5; due 9/10

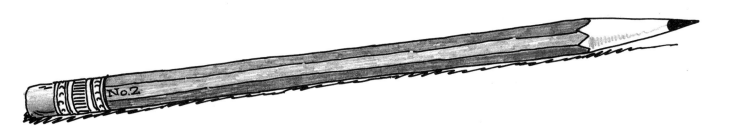

DAILY LOG

Date	Name	Assignments and Class Activities

A WORD ABOUT SEATING CHARTS

Seating charts are a necessity and, fortunately, do not take much of your time to make. You may want to reproduce two blank seating chart forms per class from the master form on the following page. Circulate one on which students can write (print) their first and last names in the appropriate squares and one on which you can legibly rewrite the students' names, if necessary. (Substitutes often have a difficult time reading some students' names if they are unfamiliar with their penmanship.)

Before using copies of the following seating chart form, make a mark in all spaces that do not apply to your classroom arrangement of seats or desks. You may want to point out the correct space for the first student to complete as the chart will appear backwards to the students.

SUGGESTIONS

◆ Staple each class's chart onto the inside of a color-coded file folder. Chronologically arrange all of your classes' file folders in a paper organizer placed on or near your desk. Each time you have a special paper or message to deliver to a student, file it in the correct class folder. If you do this, you will always have available any messages for students when you take roll.

◆ Consider letting students sit wherever they wish at the beginning of the class. Tell them they can remain in their chosen seats as long as they do not disrupt the learning atmosphere. You will be the judge of when that occurs, and your decision is final. You retain the right to move any student to a seat of your choice for the remainder of the term. When students are initially given the opportunity to choose their seat assignments, they rarely complain when moved to another seat as they know they are responsible for the move—not you.

◆ Use pencil to rewrite the final copy of the seating chart. It is easy to erase pencil marks if students change their assigned seats.

SEATING CHART

Teacher _____ **Period** _____ **Class** _____ **Room** _____

Teaching for Learning Success, Rev. Ed.

BULLETIN BOARDS:
Help or Hassle?

Bulletin boards can enhance your classroom's learning atmosphere and cause students to become more involved with classroom activities, but they can be time-consuming to construct. The information on the following pages is intended to help you make your bulletin boards successful learning tools that are easy to assemble.

There are three general types of bulletin boards. Alternate your use of these types to maintain student interest.

Permanent Bulletin Boards

Permanent bulletin boards remain virtually the same throughout the school year, although you may occasionally need to add or delete a few items. Depending on your needs, you may have two or more permanent bulletin board displays in your classroom.

- ◆ On one board, place large laminated calendars (labeled and color-coded) on which to post assignments (see page 133).

- ◆ Designate one board for the posting of classroom rules, discipline steps, grading procedures, student grade sheets, daily announcements, etc.

Working Bulletin Boards

These bulletin boards require some student interaction such as writing responses, matching or moving items, or adding pictures or information of their own choosing.

- ◆ One such display might be a "captions" bulletin board:
  - Collect interesting pictures from magazines or newspapers that lend themselves to humorous one-line captions.
  - Use pockets for student response papers (see instructions, page 145).
  - Week 1: Students suggest captions for the picture.
  - Week 2: Compile the suggestions onto one piece of paper and post it below the picture.
  - Week 3: Change the picture.

- ◆ Assemble interactive content-based bulletin boards. These boards will change when your unit of study changes.

Display Bulletin Boards

These bulletin boards are intended primarily for visual displays and providing information on particular units of study.

SUGGESTIONS FOR ALL TYPES OF BULLETIN BOARDS

◆ Use burlap or another fabric to cover bulletin boards; these materials do not fade as quickly as paper and can be reused many times. Other materials that work well are wrapping paper, newsprint, and textured material.

◆ Use staples whenever possible; straight pins or tacks are easily removed and can be dangerous in the classroom.

◆ Ready-made borders, letters, and numbers are well worth the cost as they will save you a great deal of time. They are available from most educational supply stores or catalogs.

◆ Use bright colors on your bulletin boards whenever possible.

◆ Use yarn to section off portions of the bulletin board or to connect items.

◆ Depending on the age of your students, involve them as much as possible in the construction of the bulletin boards. Consider assigning teams of students to specific weeks of each month.

◆ When centering captions or titles:

   1. Measure the width of the caption and place a pin on the board at the caption's halfway point.

   2. Place the entire caption on a table.

   3. Determine the middle letter or space of the caption.

   4. Staple the letter, or the two letters on either side of the middle space, at the marked halfway point on the board.

   5. Staple the remaining letters to the board, working from the middle out toward both sides.

◆ When placing letters or papers in a horizontal line:

   1. Measure down from the top of the board on the left and right sides; place a straight pin at the points on both the left and right side of the board where you would like the tops of the letters or papers to be. Arrange the letters or papers along these marks. (For placing letters or papers in a vertical line, measure in from the left or right side at two different points near the top and bottom of the board; place a straight pin on the board at the points where you would like the sides of the letters or papers to be.)

   2. Measure a piece of string or yarn that is long enough to reach between the two straight pins. Add 6 inches to this length and cut.

   3. Tie a knot in one end of the yarn and pin the knot to the board at one of the designated pin points. Stretch the string across (or down) to the other pin and wrap it several times around the pin to fasten it. Use the string as a guide for placement of the papers.

◆ When making Working Bulletin Boards:

- Discuss student rules for use of these bulletin boards. Remind students to use only appropriate language and pictures (no racial, religious, ethnic, sexual, etc., slurs allowed).

- Use sealed, legal-size envelopes or small manila envelopes cut in half to make pockets to hold blank slips of paper for students' written responses and/or pockets to hold completed student work. Staple the envelopes around the edges to hold them in place on the board. Label the fronts of the envelopes "Blank Paper" and "Responses." Fill blank paper pocket.

- Supply pieces of yarn in the pocket for student use when connecting words, pictures, etc.

A POTPOURRI TABLE:
A Place for Everything, and Everything in Its Place

Do you ever find yourself wondering where to store items and papers that your students use frequently?

If so, you may want to add to your classroom a potpourri table on which to place odds and ends. Place the table in the front of the room, out of the direct line of traffic but easily accessible to students. A potpourri table filled with extra student handouts not only keeps you organized but will prevent you from wasting your time searching for a handout each time a student loses one. Include any or all of the following items on your potpourri table:

- ◆ paper organizer to hold folders for returning student papers (one file folder per class, labeled and color-coded) Consider the type of paper holder that files folders in a vertical "step" style.

- ◆ shallow box to hold extra handouts

- ◆ daily log binder (see pages 138–140)

- ◆ several copies of blank student assignment sheets (see page 136)

- ◆ several copies of blank monthly student calendars (see page 135)

- ◆ several copies of blank grade sheets (see page 163) or grade record sheets (see page 165)

- ◆ several copies of the "Super Note-taking System" (see pages 228–231)

- ◆ several copies of the "Study Smart Vocabulary" forms (see pages 248–250)

- ◆ scratch paper (Use the blank side of discarded handouts.)

- ◆ three-hole punch

- ◆ stapler

- ◆ a can of pencils and pens (Ask students to return these at the end of each class.)

- ◆ box of tissues

TEXTBOOK CHECKOUT

It is important to keep a record of textbooks assigned to individual students.

Checking out textbooks to students is simple if you have established an organized procedure. Make one copy of the textbook checkout list on the following page for each class or course. Use highlighters to color code each class. The diagonal lines provide space for the name or publisher of each text. Record the book numbers in the appropriate columns. If your school requires you to charge students for book damages, make note of the condition of each book when assigning it to a student. Record the book's condition in the same rectangle as the book number by using a code:

E = Excellent, **G** = Good, **F** = Fair, **P** = Poor.

If you change rooms during the day, keep a copy of this form in the folder you carry with you to each classroom. It will save you the trouble of returning to your office if a student checks out a textbook during that class period.

TEXTBOOK CHECKOUT LIST

Class _____ **Period** _____

Teacher _____

Student Name						
1.						
2.						
3.						
4.						
5.						
6.						
7.						
8.						
9.						
10.						
11.						
12.						
13.						
14.						
15.						
16.						
17.						
18.						
19.						
20.						
21.						
22.						
23.						
24.						
25.						
26.						
27.						
28.						
29.						
30.						
31.						
32.						
33.						
34.						
35.						
36.						
37.						
38.						
39.						
40.						
41.						
42.						
43.						
44.						
45.						

Teaching for Learning Success, Rev. Ed.

ORGANIZING YOUR STUDENTS

ORGANIZING YOUR STUDENTS:
An Overview

Students need to be organized to learn effectively and efficiently. If a systematic plan of organization is instituted in your classroom, students can concentrate more on learning and will experience greater success in school. To encourage students to strive for excellence, make it easier for them to be organized by using the ideas and reproducible forms in this chapter. The information on the following pages will save you and your students time and increase effective learning.

Remember, more learning is lost through a lack of organization than through a lack of information.

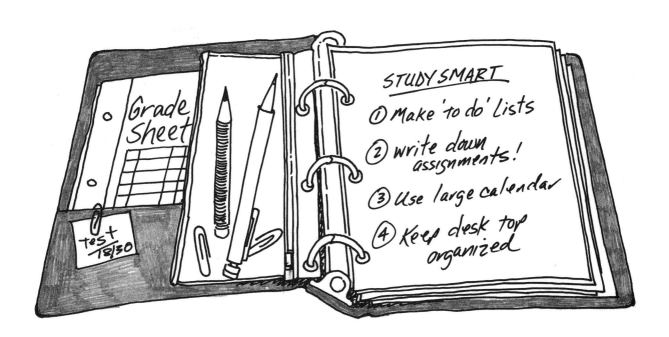

BACK-TO-SCHOOL REMINDERS

The outline on the following page provides students with organizational and planning tips that were designed to help make their school year as successful as possible. Discuss these ideas with students early in the year.

You may want to show students the outline on page 153 as an overhead transparency or an individual handout. Add to the page any additional tips or materials specific to your class, such as:

◆ "After covering textbooks, write the name of the class on the spine of each book, as well as on its front, as books are often stacked in lockers or desks, and their fronts are covered. Having the book's subject written on its spine will enable you to grab the right book every time. Use a different color-coded shape combined with the titles. For example, •*math*."

◆ "Write the titles of your classes on the spines and fronts of your three-ring binders. Use different colors and shapes for each subject."

◆ "Whenever possible, color-code book covers, spiral notebooks, ink color, labels, and tabs, using one color per class. For example, your language arts textbook cover, the cover of your language arts spiral notebook, and tabs used as section dividers in your three-ring language arts binder could be yellow."

◆ "Write your locker location, number, and combination on a 3" x 5" card and give it to your parent(s) in case they need to retrieve something for you when you are absent. It is also a good idea to copy your daily schedule on a 3" x 5" card and give it to your parent(s) in case they need to locate you during school hours. Be sure to include on the card the time of each class along with the period and simple directions for the location of each classroom and the teacher's name."

Teaching for Learning Success, Rev. Ed.

BACK-TO-SCHOOL REMINDERS

ORGANIZE YOUR LOCKER

◆ Include in your locker:

  • shelf organizer

  • message board (dry-erase board or post-it notes)

  • calendar

  • copy of your daily schedule

  • calculator

  • small amount of money

  • extra paper, pens, pencils, white-out, tissue paper, tape, computer discs, etc.

  • magnetic locker door boxes

◆ Plan ahead—take enough textbooks and materials for two or three classes.

◆ Do not visit your locker between each class.

◆ Do not give your locker combination to anyone!

ORGANIZE YOURSELF IN CLASS

◆ Find two "study-buddies" per class. Be sure to get their phone numbers.

◆ Record your assignments in an assignment notebook or assignment sheet.

◆ Arrive as early as possible to each class. Be prepared to listen and take notes from the very beginning of class.

◆ Know classroom rules and organization.

◆ Use three-ring binders divided into sections with colored tabs. Include extra paper, pockets for handouts, a plastic zipper bag for pens, pencils, etc.

ORGANIZING YOUR NOTEBOOK

Remember the 10-second rule: If you can't find what you are looking for in 10 seconds, you lose your focus. Keeping your notebook organized will help you to study and learn effectively.

- Why a 3-ring binder is best:
    - Allows for easy addition and/or deletion of papers
    - Allows for rearrangement of papers
    - Keeps papers securely
    - Allows for color-coded, tabbed section dividers
    - Provides storage for needed supplies
- Write your name, street, phone number, and email address in a prominent location.
- Use a 3-hole plastic/cloth pouch in each binder for general supplies.
    - Consider class subjects in binder when selecting supplies.
- Use assignment sheets:
    - Keep 5–10 blank sheets in a pocket of the binder you use first each day.
    - Begin with a new assignment sheet each day.
    - Combine all your classes on one sheet.
- Use a portable 3-hole punch for handouts:
    - Immediately use it if necessary for handouts/loose papers.
    - Place handout in correct section of notebook to avoid losing papers.
- Use colored divider pages:
    - Assign a different color for each subject.
    - Place clear tabs behind each colored tab divider and label them:
        - Class notes
        - Handouts
        - Homework
        - Add any extras as needed: lab (science), writing projects (language arts), maps (geography), etc.
    - Consider special, labeled sections for:
        - Class requirements/rules
        - Monthly calendars
        - Lists of classmates and phone/email information
        - Extra notebook paper

STUDENT INVENTORY CARDS

WHAT

◆ This is a simple card system that provides up-to-date, pertinent information on every student.

WHY

◆ This system provides an easy method of getting to know students as soon as possible.

◆ The cards provide easy access to general student information such as student and parent names, phone numbers, class schedules, etc.

◆ It is a flexible system which allows information to be easily amended.

◆ Using student inventory cards is the first step to setting up a parent/student phone log for school/home communication.

HOW

◆ Distribute two 3" x 5" index cards to each student during the first week of class. (Keep one set of cards at school and one at home.)

◆ Explain to the students your reasons for gathering the information. Remind them to inform you if any of this information changes throughout the school year so that you can update the cards.

◆ Display the master form (found on the following page) on an overhead projector and review the format students should follow to complete their cards.

- Instruct students to print only.

- Ask for questions.

- Allow sufficient time for completion of cards.

- Collect all cards.

- Alphabetize cards.

- Separate cards into two piles.

- Keep one set of cards at school and one at home. Use index card boxes with color-coded tabs to separate each class.

Name: **Brittany Noble**
Phone Number: **555-1476**
Phone Number (list a second number, if necessary):

Father's Name: **David Noble**
Mother's Name: **Jennifer**   Work Phone: **555-2659**
                                     Work Phone:
Address: **1425 Ventura Blvd.
Monterey, CA**   Address: (if you have a second residence)

Birth Date: **April 4th**
Hobbies: **roller skating, reading**

Favorite School Subjects: **English, lunch**

- After all student and class changes are made to the cards, copy appropriate information into your parent/student phone log.

STUDENT INVENTORY CARD

FRONT

Name:

Phone Number:

Phone Number (list a second number, if necessary):

Father's Name:	Work Phone:	Cell:
Mother's Name:	Work Phone:	Cell:

Address: Address: (if you have a second residence)

Birth Date:

Hobbies:

Favorite School Subjects:

BACK

Daily Schedule:

Class: Period: Teacher:

Locker #:   Location of Locker:

CLASS DIRECTORY AND STUDY GROUP INVENTORY

Reproduce a copy of the class directory and study group inventory form (found on the following page) for each student in your class. This form provides students with a quick reference for phone contacts and names when forming study groups or trying to locate missed assignments.

Hold a short class discussion on the merits of study groups, their purpose, and their outcome. For many students, the idea of forming a study group is a new one. Make this inventory optional.

CLASS DIRECTORY AND STUDY GROUP INVENTORY

Class/Course _____ **Time/Period** _____

Name	Phone number, if you would like it published in the class directory.	Are you interested in being part of a study group? Yes No
1.		
2.		
3.		
4.		
5.		
6.		
7.		
8.		
9.		
10.		
11.		
12.		
13.		
14.		
15.		
16.		
17.		
18.		
19.		
20.		
21.		
22.		
23.		
24.		
25.		
26.		
27.		
28.		
29.		
30.		

Teaching for Learning Success, Rev. Ed.

STUDENT GRADE SHEETS AND RECORDS

The following pages contain instructions for the use of grade sheets and records, as well as handouts on which students can keep ongoing lists of their grades. Asking students to keep track of their own grades prevents them from taking up your teaching time with continuous requests to find out their grades and keep them informed of daily and weekly progress.

The student grade sheet on page 163 allows students to keep track of grades that have been issued using a point system. Teacher instructions on the use of this form are included (page 160), as are reproducible student instructions (pages 161–162). Provide each student with one copy of the student instructions and suggest that they store the instructions in their binders for quick reference when averaging their grades. The student grade record form on page 165 provides students with a method of keeping track of assignments that have been scored with letter grades instead of points.

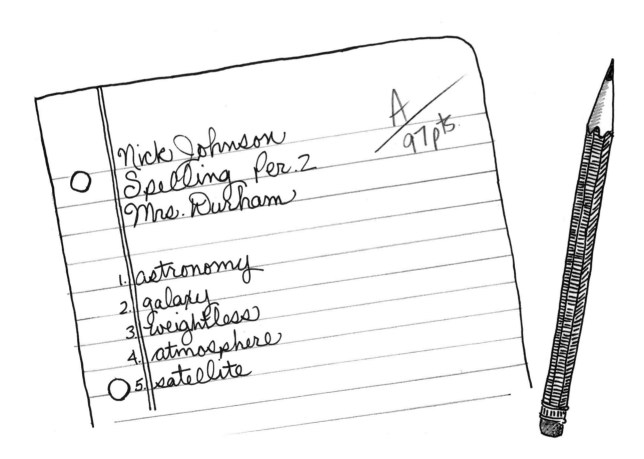

STUDENT GRADE SHEETS

WHY

- Student grade sheets make students responsible for keeping track of their own grades.

- Student grade sheets prevent students from taking your time to ask for updates of their averages.

- The grade sheets help students identify missing assignments.

- They help parents stay abreast of their child's daily progress.

HOW

1. Duplicate and post in the classroom one sample student grade sheet (page 163) for each class taught. This sample will serve as a guide for all students to follow. When you make each assignment or hand it back, fill in the student grade sheet with the basic information.

2. Distribute the student grade sheet instructions (pages 161–162) and the student grade sheet form (page 163) to students after returning their first graded assignment.

3. Discuss with students the importance of keeping track of their own grades.

4. Review with students the steps to follow listed on their instruction sheets.

5. Help students enter the first assignment on their grade sheets.

6. Review each student's grade sheet to assess whether it has been completed correctly.

7. Remind students that they are responsible for keeping track of their grades throughout the grading period.

8. Point out to students the master grade sheet posted in the classroom that will contain the correct listing of all assignments, their due dates, assignment numbers and titles, and points possible.

9. **Optional:** You may want to award points or a grade for maintaining a complete and up-to-date grade sheet.

HOW TO USE
STUDENT GRADE SHEETS

Each time a graded assignment is returned to you, you will enter the information for each assignment on your student grade sheet.

1. Record the date the assignment is due in the "Date" column.

2. Record the assignment number in the "Assignment Number" column.

3. Record the title or name of the assignment in the "Assignment Title" column. When in doubt, check the master grade sheet posted in the classroom.

4. Record the total number of possible points for the assignment in the "Points Possible" column.

5. Record the total number of points you received on the assignment in the "Points Earned" column.

6. Add the number of points you earned on this assignment to the number of total points in the "Total Points" column. This is a running total of points for the entire grading period, not just for this assignment.

7. Compute the percent you earned on this assignment by dividing the number of possible points into the number of points you earned on this assignment and multiplying your result by 100. Write this percent in the "Percent" column.

8. Using your teacher's grade point distribution scale for the class (for example: 93%–100% = A, 90%–92% = A–, etc.), record the letter grade, if applicable, in the "Grade" column.

9. You can compute your overall grade for the class at any time by adding the total number of possible points in the "Points Possible" column and dividing that number into the last number entered in the "Total Points" column (the actual points you have earned in the class). Multiply your result by 100. This will give you your overall percentage for assignments in the class.

10. Remember, this is only the grade for all *assignments*. There may be other considerations that affect your final grade, such as participation and attitude points, attendance points, and extra credit points. Ask your teacher for this information.

11. Test grades may or may not be included on this form. Ask your teacher.

EXAMPLE:

Date	Assignment Number	Assignment Title	Points Possible	Points Earned	Total Points	Percent*	Grade
9/26	# 1	*Types of Triangles* *p. 27 #3 – 38*	50	47		94%	A

Note: Because this is the first assignment, there are no other points to add to the 47 points in the "Points Earned" column. However, the points earned for the second assignment would be added to the 47 points recorded in this column. All future points earned would be added in the same way.

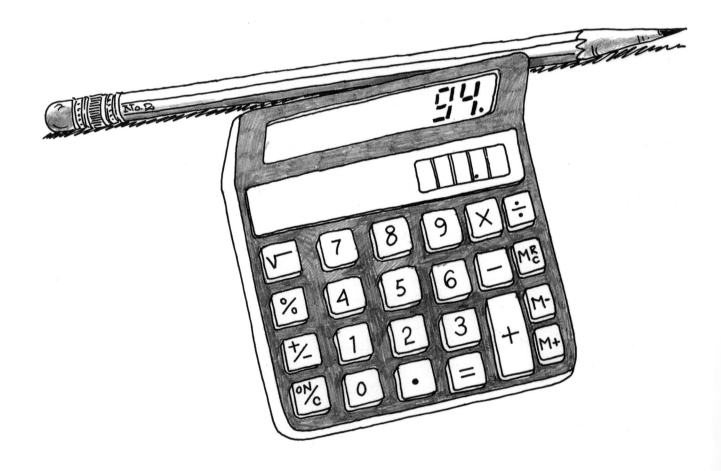

Teaching for Learning Success, Rev. Ed.

STUDENT GRADE SHEET

Class _____ **Teacher** _____ **Name** _____

Date	Assignment Number	Assignment Title	Points Possible	Points Earned	Total Points	Percent	Grade

STUDENT GRADE RECORDS

If students receive letter grades instead of points, they should use the student grade record form on the following page to calculate their overall grades. This form also charts weighted grades. (If quizzes and tests are weighted differently than daily assignments, the student enters the amount of the weight in column 3.) Give students the instructions on pages 161 and 162 when filling out this form. Specific directions for calculating a letter grade are provided on the bottom of the form (page 165).

Teaching for Learning Success, Rev. Ed.

STUDENT GRADE RECORD

Name _____ Class _____ Period _____

Assignment Description	1 Grade	2 Value	3 Weight	4 Total		Grade Value	
						A+	13
						A	12
						A−	11
						B+	10
						B	9
						B−	8
						C+	7
						C	6
						C−	5
						D+	4
						D	3
						D−	2
						F	1
						0	0

To Average Your Grade:

1. Multiply the value of the grade (column 2) by the weight of the grade (column 3). Write your result in the "Total Points" column (column 4).

2. Add the total number of points in column 3.

3. Add the total number of points in column 4.

4. Subtract any necessary points for tardies, unexcused absences, or not being prepared from the total number of points in column 4.

5. Divide this figure by the total number of points in column 3.

6. Find the letter equivalent to your numerical average on the grade values chart. (.6 and above are rounded up to the next whole number.)

Teaching for Learning Success, Rev. Ed.

©2004 by Incentive Publications, Inc., Nashville, TN.
*Acknowledgement of credit is made to
Carolyn M. Lazar-Kronke for the above material.*

GRADE REPORTS

The grade report form is an invaluable tool for calculating midterm, quarter, or semester grades. It takes very little time and effort to administer and produces a number of positive results. This grade report places the responsibility of assessment initially on the students and thus makes them more aware of their learning capabilities. The form may be used independently or in conjunction with a grade printout for each student.

Students complete the form and then submit it to you for comments and initials, indicating your agreement. This method of assessment helps students focus on specific aspects of their learning and provides an opportunity for you to briefly conference with all students concerning their progress. As you view the forms, make sure every student has correctly circled the appropriate grading period at the top of the first page and filled in his or her overall grade. Students should take the forms home for parental discussion and signatures. Because the assessment is specific, parents can discuss with their child areas of success and those which need improvement.

When students return the reports, check them for any information that might have been changed without your approval, and make note of any comments that require action. Follow through with necessary phone calls or contacts. Keep these forms on file for future reference. If parents wish to keep one, make a copy for your files and return the original to the parents.

Teaching for Learning Success, Rev. Ed.

GRADE REPORT

___ MIDTERM   ___ QUARTER   ___ SEMESTER

Name _____ Class _____ Date _____

No comment from teacher means teacher agrees with student evaluation.

I have reviewed this report _____   My grade for this class is _____

SELF-ASSESSMENT	TEACHER ASSESSMENT

ACADEMIC: _____% of final grade

1. Calculate your grade from your own records:_____
   Is it up _____ down _____ the same _____?
2. Do you have any missing work? yes_____ no_____
   If so, list the missing assignments:

   _____

   _____

   _____

3. When I am absent I:
   _____ contact the teacher and make up the work promptly
   _____ wait so long that results are poor
   _____ wait until the teacher contacts me
4. Evaluate your study habits and preparation for
   tests/quizzes:
   _____ I study 10–15 minutes per day plus homework.
   _____ I write things down when I study.
   _____ I study mostly the night before a test.
   _____ I don't study very much.

HOMEWORK: _____% of final grade

1. I do my homework: 2. I apply good study habits:
   _____ all of the time   _____ all of the time
   _____ most of the time   _____ most of the time
   _____ occasionally   _____ occasionally
   _____ rarely   _____ rarely

3. I have a set study time: _____ yes _____ no

PARTICIPATION: _____% of final grade

1. I try to participate in class:
   _____ as often as possible
   _____ several times a class period
   _____ occasionally
   _____ from time to time
   _____ I'm not comfortable raising my hand and/or
   rarely participate.
2. If you have trouble participating, have you worked with
   the teacher to develop a participation plan?
   _____ yes _____ no

*Note: Poor homework and participation grades can lower
final grade.*

©2004 by Incentive Publications, Inc., Nashville, TN.
*Acknowledgement of credit is made to
Carolyn M. Lazar-Kronke for the above material.*

SELF-ASSESSMENT	**TEACHER ASSESSMENT**

GENERAL ATTITUDE:

1. In class I am attentive and on-task:

_____ always   _____ often

_____ occasionally   _____ rarely

2. I take notes when appropriate: yes   no

3. I write down assignments: yes   no

4. My behavior in class is:

_____ polite and considerate

_____ occasionally distracting

_____ disruptive and/or rude

5. I ask for help from the teacher when I need it:

_____ yes   _____ no   _____ sometimes

6. I take advantage of tutoring when offered:

_____ yes   _____ no

7. I am pleased with my effort and performance in this class:

_____ yes   _____ no

8. If the answer to #7 is no, how do you plan to improve?
   Be specific:

_____

_____

_____

ATTENDANCE:

1. I am absent: 2. I am tardy

_____ rarely/never   _____ rarely/never

_____ occasionally   _____ occasionally

_____ often (number of   _____ often (number of

   times:_____)   times:_____)

Note: Excessive absences or tardies can affect your grade.

Student Signature _____ Date _____

Parent Signature _____ Date _____

I would like to:

_____ schedule a conference

_____ speak with you on the phone   work # _____ home # _____

Comments: _____

_____

_____

_____

_____

©2004 by Incentive Publications, Inc., Nashville, TN.
*Acknowledgement of credit is made to
Carolyn M. Lazar-Kronke for the above material.*

Teaching for Learning Success, Rev. Ed.

HOME STUDY TIME

While each of us has unique study habits, there are some general rules about studying that apply to everyone. One is that the brain can concentrate for only a certain amount of time before it needs a break. This time spent in concentration is called focused attention span. For a person in grades 6–9, the focused attention span for learning new information is about 37 minutes. This means that a person in these grades can study for up to 37 minutes before needing a short break. For a person in grades 10 and up, the focused attention span is about 47 minutes.

Understanding how the brain processes information can help students plan their study time more wisely. If students study without distractions for 30 minutes, take a 10 minute break (leave their desks/rooms and do something physical), and then return for another 30 minutes of studying, they will be using their brain power effectively. After using this study plan for two weeks, students will notice that they accomplish twice as much in half the amount of time. At the beginning of each 30-minute session, set a realistic goal for the work to be completed in that time period.

Use the following page as a handout or as a transparency displayed on the overhead projector when discussing with students how to study more efficiently. Students will be amazed at the difference this method can make in the effective use of their study time! Younger students should vary the schedule; for example, students in grades 3–5 may want to study for 20 minutes, take a 10 minute break, and return to the books for 20 more minutes. The habit is what is important! A good rule to follow is 10 minutes per grade level five nights a week as a minimum study time. Example: 8th grade = 80 minutes, five nights a week.

When discussing efficient study habits, stress to students that distractions are the leading cause of poor concentration. Impress upon your students that they should study at their desk or in their room by themselves and practice the 30/10/30 study method.

STUDY TIME...

☐ **30**

☐ **10**

☐ **30**

STUDY SMART

——— Checklist ———

**Make the most of your time and effort
when studying.**

Here's how:

- ◆ Organize your time and materials.

- ◆ Set priorities and follow through with them.

- ◆ Employ good reading skills.

- ◆ Always understand why you need to learn, and use an appropriate, organized system to learn.

- ◆ Concentrate! Intend to learn and remember information when you begin studying.

- ◆ Use good note-taking skills and make study sheets.

- ◆ Be an active learner in class and at home.

- ◆ Turn in organized and neat assignments.

- ◆ Constantly review.

- ◆ Form study groups, and seek help when needed.

- ◆ Use all of your senses to learn.

VOUCHERS FOR ASSIGNMENT EXEMPTION

WHAT

♦ This system allows for an assignment to be replaced with a voucher. Each student is given a set number of vouchers for the semester or grading period to be used on only those assignments noted by the teacher.

♦ Vouchers count neither for or against the total grade.

WHY

♦ Vouchers provide a safeguard for students who occasionally forget to complete or turn in an assignment.

♦ Vouchers demonstrate that you understand students' occasional oversights and are somewhat forgiving, even with a policy that strictly forbids late work.

♦ Vouchers are foolproof and easy to record and track.

HOW

♦ Copy the vouchers on pages 173–174 and duplicate enough for your classes. You may want to reproduce them on colored paper so that they are easily distinguishable from your other papers. Two vouchers per grading period per student is recommended.

♦ Explain the following rules to students:

  • Every student will receive 2 vouchers which are valid only until _____ .

  • Extra vouchers will not be given; so if these are lost, they are gone for good!

  • Students should write their name and the class title on each voucher.

  • A voucher may be used in place of certain assignments during this grading period. When an assignment is given, the teacher will tell students if they can or cannot use a voucher for that particular assignment. (Optional: Vouchers may not be used for major projects, quizzes, or tests.)

  • Vouchers are recorded in the gradebook in place of the assignment. A voucher simply excuses a student from that particular assignment; the assignment's points or grade is not lost or gained.

  • Vouchers are recorded in the gradebook by completely darkening in the square for that assignment so that it will be very easy to spot, and will show immediately when a student has handed in all possible vouchers for a grading period.

  • Additional vouchers will not be accepted.

  • Optional: For every voucher not used at the end of the grading period, extra credit points will be awarded.

  • Vouchers must be handed in at the same time the assignment is collected.

  • New vouchers will be distributed each grading period.

Teaching for Learning Success, Rev. Ed.

Voucher

Name _____

Date _____ Class _____ Period _____

Assignment _____

_____

_____

_____

_____

_____

_____

_____

_____

_____

_____

VOUCHER

NAME _____

DATE _____ CLASS _____ PERIOD _____

ASSIGNMENT _____

_____

_____

_____

_____

_____

_____

_____

_____

_____

_____

_____

_____

_____

Teaching for Learning Success, Rev. Ed.

INVOLVING PARENTS

INVOLVING PARENTS:

An Overview

You may have to work hard to receive parental support, but you will find that your efforts will be worthwhile. The benefits of positive parental involvement and continuous school-home communication are successful students, happy parents, and motivated teachers. Unfortunately, the power of the school-home connection is often overlooked by teachers who consider the benefits not worth the effort. Don't let this happen to you!

The following pages provide tips and advice for including parents in your curriculum. A variety of highly successful plans, parent letters, and master forms are ready to copy and send home to parents. Do not forget to give a copy of everything you send to your students' parents to your principal! Always keep your administration informed and involved.

Note to Teachers:

The following pages can be used in a variety of ways:

- ◆ to include with information sent home during the first week of school

- ◆ to use as overhead transparencies and/or handouts for Back-to-School Night

- ◆ to include with monthly newsletters or weekly student take-home folders

- ◆ to use as handouts distributed during parent-teacher conferences

- ◆ to accompany appropriate long- or short-term student assignments

PARENT LETTERS:

Keeping Them Informed

Every teacher wants and functions best with parental support. To achieve parental support, the teacher must take the first step. Since parental support can flourish only through good school-home communications, it is necessary to provide continual avenues for communication between yourself and your students' parents. For the relationship to be successful, the system you institute needs to be organized and easy to administer. The use of parent letters is one highly successful method.

The information on the following pages outlines specific strategies for instituting and administering a variety of parent letters. "The First Parent Newsletter" (pages 179–180) offers suggestions for your first newsletter's format and content, including information on your expectations, classroom rules, grading system, and more. The reproducible parent letter (page 183) informs parents of your intent to occasionally send home study skills strategies and hints for them as well as their children. This letter can be sent home at the beginning of the school year. The monthly newsletter (refer to sample on page 184) extends school-home communications by presenting parents with a simple procedure to help them stay informed of your classroom progress on a monthly basis.

Keeping parents informed through letters increases their support of your classroom methods. They will feel a part of their children's school lives and thus more likely to extend help to you when you need it.

SUGGESTIONS

- ◆ Always give your principal or other administrators a copy of your newsletter. (They will be impressed by your organization and thoughtfulness!)

- ◆ Notify parents when they should expect these letters (the first school day of every month, for example).

- ◆ Keep an extra copy of each newsletter in your files.

- ◆ Slip a few extra copies of each newsletter in the extra handouts box on your potpourri table.

THE FIRST PARENT NEWSLETTER

WHAT

- ◆ The first parent newsletter initiates school-home communication early in the school year.
- ◆ It incorporates a short statement of your teaching philosophy and expectations, describes your room rules, discipline system, and grading system, and informs parents about your classroom procedures.
- ◆ Your first parent newsletter should be sent home within the first few days of class.
- ◆ It serves as a substitute for the monthly parent newsletter.

WHY

- ◆ It demonstrates organization and thorough planning.
- ◆ It provides you, your students, and their parents with a common definition of classroom procedures and expectations.
- ◆ It informs your principal that you have made early and positive contact with parents.
- ◆ It provides concrete proof to parents, students, and principal that everyone was informed in writing of your classroom procedures and rules in a timely manner. A parental signature on the newsletter also proves that parents were informed of your rules.

MATERIALS

- ◆ computer and printer or a typewriter
- ◆ paper and pen
- ◆ school calendar (if you refer to any important dates)
- ◆ copies of room rules, class schedule, grading system, etc.

HOW

1. You may want to use a border and graphics or pictures throughout the newsletter to attract more interest to your letter and make it unique.

2. Date it and use a friendly salutation with which you are comfortable.

3. Begin with a brief welcome statement, and state the title, level of your class, and reason for sending this letter.

4. Include the following in your letter: (Use bulleted lists whenever possible to make it brief, simple, and direct.)
   - your philosophy
   - your expectations regarding assignments, homework, activity outcomes, and general student behavior in the classroom
   - your policies on classroom rules, discipline procedures, homework, late papers, grading system, when parents can expect regular communications from you, and student materials you require (notebooks, binders, etc.).

THE FIRST PARENT NEWSLETTER

5. Include a brief outline of units or concepts to be covered during the first month of school and list any important upcoming deadlines.

6. Inform parents where and when you may be reached to answer questions and/or receive their comments (regular office hours, by appointment only, etc.).

7. Personally sign the letter.

8. Draw a dotted line (along which to tear) and beneath the dotted line write: "I have read the above information regarding policies and procedures for Mr./Mrs./Ms. (your last name)'s (title of class)."

9. Leave two labeled spaces at the bottom of the letter for parent(s) and students to sign. Leave one space for the date. Write a note explaining that parents may keep the letter for future reference but must return the signature portion of the letter. Follow up to make sure all parents and students read, sign, and return their signatures to you.

IN CLASS

1. Give students time in class to carefully read this letter; discuss any questions they might have.

2. Have students sign the letter.

3. Inform students that they are to take the letter home, discuss it with their parents, have their parents sign it, and return it to you.

4. Tell them the date on which you expect it returned.

5. Write this assignment on the master assignment calendar (see page 133).

6. Instruct students to write the date on which the letter is to be returned on their student calendars (see page 134).

7. File a copy of the letter for your own reference.

8. File all portions of returned letters.

9. It is very important that all letters are returned. For those students who forget to return it, you might:

   • Tell them that you are recording their grades in pencil and that they will become final grades only when the signature portion of the letter is returned.

   • Call home and talk with the students' parents.

   • Have the students write daily letters (on their own time) as reminders to themselves.

10. Don't forget to give a copy of the letter to your teammates, principal, other administrators, counselors, etc., for their reference.

PARENT LETTER AND MONTHLY NEWSLETTER

PARENT LETTER

The parent letter on page 183 can be sent home at the beginning of the year to explain your intent of occasionally supplying students with handouts and ideas for learning strategies in connection with regular assignments. You may reproduce the letter as is or change it to better fit your personal needs. You might add to the bottom of the letter a line on which parents can sign and date the letter if you want it returned.

For additional reproducible forms containing parental communication as well as student study skills and strategies, refer to *Learning to Learn: Strengthening Study Skills and Brain Power, Revised Edition,* by Gloria Frender. Incentive Publications: Nashville, TN, 2004.

MONTHLY NEWSLETTER

WHAT

♦ The monthly newsletter is a letter sent home to parents via their children that informs and updates parents regarding classroom activities, assignments, and curriculum. This is appropriate for all grade levels.

WHY

♦ It provides a monthly opportunity for you to reexamine your plans for every class.

♦ It is an extremely effective tool that increases school-home communication.

♦ By giving your principal a copy of your monthly newsletter, he or she will be continually updated on your classroom activities; this improves your communication with the administration.

♦ The letter gives students the responsibility of informing parents of your activities.

♦ It allows parents to plan dental and doctor's appointments around important dates listed in the newsletter.

♦ It allows you to ask for parental help with particular problems. For example, "In the last week I've noticed too many mechanical errors on final writing papers. Try to encourage your children to proofread their work more thoroughly."

♦ Parents like being informed of their children's school activities.

♦ Regular communication encourages strong parental support for your program.

♦ It encourages parents to work with you for the benefit of the students.

PARENT LETTER AND MONTHLY NEWSLETTER

 ◆ It shows students that parents will always be informed of your classroom's activities.
 ◆ The space reserved for parental comments allows you to be more informed of parents' feelings and possibly ward off problems while they are still minor.
 ◆ It makes parent/teacher conferences easier and more successful.

MATERIALS

 ◆ computer and printer or a typewriter
 ◆ paper
 ◆ pen
 ◆ school calendar (if you refer to any important dates occurring that month)
 ◆ current lesson plans

HOW

1. You may want to use a border and graphics or pictures throughout the newsletter to attract more interest to your letter and make it unique.

2. Date it and use a friendly salutation with which you are comfortable.

3. Plan to distribute newsletters the first school day of each month.

4. Follow the same format throughout the year or course.

5. Write only on the front side of a page, and try to keep it to one page.

6. Always date and personally sign the letters.

7. Begin with a positive statement that refers to an event from the previous month. (For example, "Students were very enthusiastic and well informed when giving their oral reports last week.")

8. Give a brief overview of concepts and activities to be covered during the upcoming month. Whenever possible, mention specific dates, but make some allowance for units or activities that take longer to complete than anticipated.

9. Mention any concepts or activities that you did not complete during the previous month.

10. List important dates such as due dates for assignments, field trips, school holidays, and guest speakers.

11. End the newsletter with a reminder that you are always open to parental concerns and comments; include your office phone number.

12. Leave space at the bottom of the letter for student and parent signatures and comments.

13. Make the signatures and comments section detachable so that parents may keep the letter for reference but return the signature portion.

14. Write the letter in an informal and friendly manner, avoiding technical or educational jargon. See page 184 for sample monthly newsletter.

Teaching for Learning Success, Rev. Ed.

A Note from the Teacher

Dear Parents,

Real learning involves knowing how to learn as well as what to learn. It's very important for your child to acquire learning skills in addition to content in order to become a successful independent learner.

To better understand and learn this course's content, I will occasionally supply your child with helpful study skills handouts and materials that provide a variety of learning strategies. These handouts may be distributed in connection with a specific assignment or used separately.

Feel free to contact me at school concerning any comments or questions you might have.

Sincerely,

OCTOBER LANGUAGE ARTS NEWSLETTER

October 4, 2004

Dear Parents,

Please try to drop in this month to see the fantastic posters, dioramas, murals, and written reports the class completed for our mythology unit. We all had fun and learned many new concepts to apply to other areas of study.

This month our focus for expository writing will be on improving mechanics and applying some grammar rules. Commas, quotations, hyphens, subject/verb agreement, and spelling will be the target areas. Careful proofreading continues to be stressed; perhaps you could check that your student has proofread his or her assignment one last time before turning it in. Also, watch for additional vocabulary worksheets each Tuesday and Friday.

We will begin on the short stories for our literature unit in a few days. Ask your student to share some with you. We will be learning and applying specific literary vocabulary in analyzing plot and theme.

Important dates this month are:

Wednesday, October 6—*newsletter returned*

Friday, October 8—*descriptive paragraphs due*

Every Wednesday—*pre- and post-spelling tests*

Every Friday—*Vocabulary Day*

Monday, October 18—*no school*

Tuesday, October 26—*written book reviews due*

There will be other assignments due throughout the month as well. Periodically ask your student to share his or her calendar with you.

Please feel free to contact me at any time with comments, questions, or concerns at:_____

Sincerely,

_____   _____
Student Signature   Parent/Guardian Signature

Comments: _____

_____

_____

_____

_____

Teaching for Learning Success, Rev. Ed.

WEEKLY STUDENT
TAKE-HOME PACKETS

WHAT

◆ The weekly student take-home packet allows student work to be gathered each week and compiled to be sent home.

◆ Parents review the students' work, keep any papers necessary, sign the packet, and return it to school.

WHY

◆ This is an effective and efficient system to send student work home for review.

◆ The packets keep parents informed of their children's progress on a weekly basis; therefore, there will be no surprises at parent-teacher conferences or grade time.

◆ The organization of the packets allows teachers or parents to catch small problems and correct them before they become any bigger.

◆ Sending the packets to parents promotes school-home communication.

◆ Completing the packets requires very little work on your part, yet provides many advantages to students and parents.

◆ Parents respond positively to the packets, and parents and teachers are encouraged to work together for the benefit of the student.

◆ From the beginning of the year, the compilation of take-home packets entrusts students with accountability for their work.

◆ Missing assignments are readily apparent to students and their parents, as students are required to produce the assignments listed on the table of contents. Teachers and parents can intervene early when students do not complete their work.

MATERIALS

◆ labeled file folders for each student (color-coded for that class; for example, 1st period is green, 2nd period is yellow etc.)

◆ blank paper or master copy of table of contents (see page 188 and page 189)

◆ convenient place to store the table of contents so that you can add to it continually (for example, on a clip board kept on top of a filing cabinet, attached to the pull-out board in your desk, etc.)

◆ pen

◆ student-supplied folders for papers

◆ introductory parent letter to place in first take-home folder

WEEKLY STUDENT TAKE-HOME PACKETS

HOW

1. Make copies of the blank forms to use as your table of contents (see page 188 and page 189), or divide a piece of paper into sections for all classes (or one per class) to meet your needs. Be sure to leave room for parental signature and comments.

2. Store the table of contents in an accessible place so that you may add to it daily; this will serve as the master to copy for student packets.

3. Each time an assignment is made, enter its title, page number, assignment number, etc., on the table of contents form.

4. After returning and discussing corrected assignments, each student files the paper in his or her individual file folder; these folders may be kept by the students if they have an available storage space at school, or in a file cabinet drawer for that class.

5. The day before you want to send the folders home, copy your master table of contents for every student in your class.

6. Students are responsible for assembling their packets in proper order, using the table of contents as a guide. Depending on the age of the students, you may have to review this process with them the first time they are asked to complete it.

7. You might want to review assembled packets if you feel the need.

8. Students sign the packets. Their signatures indicate that they are aware of their packets' contents.

9. Each student takes home his or her packet, shares it with his or her parent(s), and collects parental signature(s).

10. Parents may keep any or all papers.

11. Students return signed packets to you.

12. Using a class list, check off each packet when it is returned. Check for parental signatures and comments. Respond accordingly.

13. Include in the first student packet the introductory parent letter on page 190, or write one of you own.

SUGGESTIONS

◆ You may want to establish a routine of assembling packets on Fridays and returning them on Mondays, as parents will have more time to review the packets on the weekend.

◆ Place a box labeled "Student Packets" in a convenient location so that students may drop them in the box when returning them. You can check the box at your convenience.

Teaching for Learning Success, Rev. Ed.

SAMPLE

TABLE OF CONTENTS

ALL SUBJECTS

Name: _Example_ Class: _5th Grade_ Period: _____

Today's Date: _10-13-04_ Return Date: _10-14-04_

1. Subject _Math_ — pg.#
   - _Long Division pg. 19_ — 1
   - _Worksheet #37_ — 2
   - _Thought Problems p. 26_ — 3

2. Subject _Lang Arts_ — pg.#
   - _Using Periods #1_ — 4
   - _Fun with Words #16_ — 5
   - _Descriptive Paragraph_ — 6
   - _Short Story Summary_ — 7

3. Subject _Social Studies_ — pg.#
   - _Map around the world_ — 8
   - _Group Activity sheet_ — 9

4. Subject _Science_ — pg.#
   - _Types of Whales #62_ — 10
   - _Baleen Whales p. 29_ — 11
   - _Notes in film_ — 12
   - _Reading Summary_ — 13

5. Subject _Music_ — pg.#
   - _What Makes a Chorus #4_ — 14

6. Subject _Art_ — pg.#
   - _Black on White Designs_ — 15

7. Subject _____ — pg.#

8. Subject _____ — pg.#

_____ Student Signature

_____ Parent/Guardian Signature

Comments: _____

TABLE OF CONTENTS

ONE SUBJECT

Name: _Example_ Class: _9th Grade L.A._ Period: _3_

Today's Date: _9-20-04_ Return Date: _9-23-04_

Content Area: _Writing_ — pg.#
Title of Assignment:
- _Writing Thesis Statements_ — 1
- _Expository paragraph: narrative_ — 2

Content Area: _Literature_ — pg.#
Title of Assignment:
- _"A Day to Remember" worksheet #14_ — 3
- _List of Literary Terms #1-20_ — 4
- _Elements of a Short Story Class notes_ — 5

Content Area: _Vocabulary_ — pg.#
Title of Assignment:
- _Lesson #1_ — 6
- _Lesson #2_ — 7

Content Area: _Spelling_ — pg.#
Title of Assignment:
- _Set #1_ — 8
- _Set #2_ — 9

_____ Student Signature

_____ Parent/Guardian Signature

Comments: _____

TABLE OF CONTENTS

ALL SUBJECTS

Name:_____ Class: _____ Period: _____

Today's Date: _____ Return Date: _____

1. Subject _____ pg.#
   _____ _____
   _____ _____
   _____ _____
   _____ _____
   _____ _____
   _____ _____

2. Subject _____ pg.#
   _____ _____
   _____ _____
   _____ _____
   _____ _____
   _____ _____
   _____ _____

3. Subject _____ pg.#
   _____ _____
   _____ _____
   _____ _____
   _____ _____
   _____ _____
   _____ _____

4. Subject _____ pg.#
   _____ _____
   _____ _____
   _____ _____
   _____ _____
   _____ _____
   _____ _____

5. Subject _____ pg.#
   _____ _____
   _____ _____
   _____ _____
   _____ _____
   _____ _____
   _____ _____

6. Subject _____ pg.#
   _____ _____
   _____ _____
   _____ _____
   _____ _____
   _____ _____
   _____ _____

7. Subject _____ pg.#
   _____ _____
   _____ _____
   _____ _____
   _____ _____
   _____ _____
   _____ _____

8. Subject _____ pg.#
   _____ _____
   _____ _____
   _____ _____
   _____ _____
   _____ _____
   _____ _____

_____   _____
Student Signature   *Parent/Guardian Signature*

Comments: _____
_____
_____
_____

TABLE OF CONTENTS

ONE SUBJECT

Name:_____ Class: _____ Period: _____

Today's Date: _____ Return Date: _____

Content Area:_____

Title of Assignment: pg.#

_____ _____

_____ _____

_____ _____

_____ _____

_____ _____

Content Area:_____

Title of Assignment: pg.#

_____ _____

_____ _____

_____ _____

_____ _____

_____ _____

Content Area:_____

Title of Assignment: pg.#

_____ _____

_____ _____

_____ _____

_____ _____

_____ _____

Content Area:_____

Title of Assignment: pg.#

_____ _____

_____ _____

_____ _____

_____ _____

_____ _____

_____   _____
Student Signature   *Parent/Guardian Signature*

Comments: _____

_____

_____

_____

Date: _____

Dear Parents,

Every Friday your student will bring home a packet of papers that includes all of the assignments completed that week. A table of contents lists all individual assignments and their page numbers. Your child will be responsible for assembling his or her folder and numbering the pages according to the table of contents.

There are two spaces at the bottom of the table of contents page: one for your signature and one for that of your child. Please sign on the appropriate line after reviewing your child's work, keep any or all of the assignments, and return the signed table of contents and folder to school with your child on Monday.

Please take time to sit down with your child to discuss his or her work. If assignments are missing, ask for an explanation. Post several assignments at home and give positive reinforcement for improvement.

These weekly folders will help keep you informed of your student's progress on a regular basis as well as keep you informed about the course content. It will help me to better communicate with you, answer any questions, or address any concerns you might have on a regular basis. Most importantly, this folder will help your student realistically measure his or her progress and become responsible for his or her own learning.

Feel free to write your comments when you return the take-home packet, or phone me at school. Thank you for taking an active part in your student's education!

Sincerely,

PARENT/STUDENT PHONE LOG

Continual school-home communication is extremely important as it provides both parents and students with positive reinforcement and can serve as effective preventive medicine when problems are just beginning. A call home during the first month of school helps demonstrate your personal interest in that student and introduces parents to a teacher who cares. Making positive comments on student progress and telling parents how much their child is appreciated in your class makes a long-lasting impression on both parents and students. Most often, any problems that need to be brought to parents' attention are easily solved if parents are informed as soon as possible. When you call a student's parents at home, briefly speak with the student on the phone, if you have not already done so in school that day. Speaking with the student before speaking with his or her parents makes the student an active participant in this three-way communication process. Begin your conversation on a positive note. Your conversation with a student might sound something like this:

"Hello, Tim, this is Mrs. Stevens. I just wanted to let you know how much I enjoy having you in class and how much I appreciate your active participation. The last writing assignment you turned in was especially good. Keep up the good work! May I speak with your Mom and Dad so that I can share this with them?"

or this:

"Hello, Sara, this is Mr. Abbot. I just wanted to let your parents know how much I enjoy having you in class. We also need to discuss your last two missing assignments. You and I talked about it today in class, but it would help you if your parents also were informed. Have you had a chance to talk with them regarding these assignments?"

Remember these rules:
1. Call at a convenient time.
2. Identify yourself (your name, student's name, the name of the class).
3. Talk to the student first.
4. Keep your conversation with parents short and to the point.
5. State the student's behavior or progress as you observe it.
6. If there is a problem, state the solution you will try in class.
7. Ask for follow-through from parents at home.
8. End the conversation with a positive statement.
9. Record the phone call and any pertinent information.

Refer to the phone log (pages 192–193) before parent-teacher conferences to remind you of previous contact with each student's parents. The phone log also serves as a great reference when seeking for information to share with team teachers or administrators needing information on a student. It is a good idea to reproduce one copy of the phone log for each class. The "Parent Name" column provides space for a mother's (M) and father's (F) names should their last names differ from those of the student. The "Telephone Number" column may be used to record home, work, and cell phone numbers or separate residence telephone numbers. There is space in the "Date" and "Comments" columns to record four telephone calls per student.

Keep all logs in one binder or folder that may be easily transported home and back to school. Periodically make copies of the logs to keep in a separate file folder in case of loss.

PARENT/STUDENT PHONE LOG

Class _____   Period _____

Student Name	Parent Name		Phone Number	Date	Comments	Date	Comments
1.	M						
	F						
2.	M						
	F						
3.	M						
	F						
4.	M						
	F						
5.	M						
	F						
6.	M						
	F						
7.	M						
	F						
8.	M						
	F						
9.	M						
	F						
10.	M						
	F						
11.	M						
	F						
12.	M						
	F						
13.	M						
	F						
14.	M						
	F						
15.	M						
	F						
16.	M						
	F						
17.	M						
	F						

Teaching for Learning Success, Rev. Ed.

Student Name		Parent Name	Phone Number	Date	Comments	Date	Comments
18.	M						
	F						
19.	M						
	F						
20.	M						
	F						
21.	M						
	F						
22.	M						
	F						
23.	M						
	F						
24.	M						
	F						
25.	M						
	F						
26.	M						
	F						
27.	M						
	F						
28.	M						
	F						
29.	M						
	F						
30.	M						
	F						
31.	M						
	F						
32.	M						
	F						
33.	M						
	F						
34.	M						
	F						
35.	M						
	F						

PARENT INVOLVEMENT

The charts on pages 195 and 196 are intended for use during back-to-school nights and/or parent-teacher conferences. Display them on an overhead projector or distribute them as handouts. The information on the charts will help parents understand the importance of parental involvement, as well as provide parents with practical and simple suggestions of ways they can help at home.

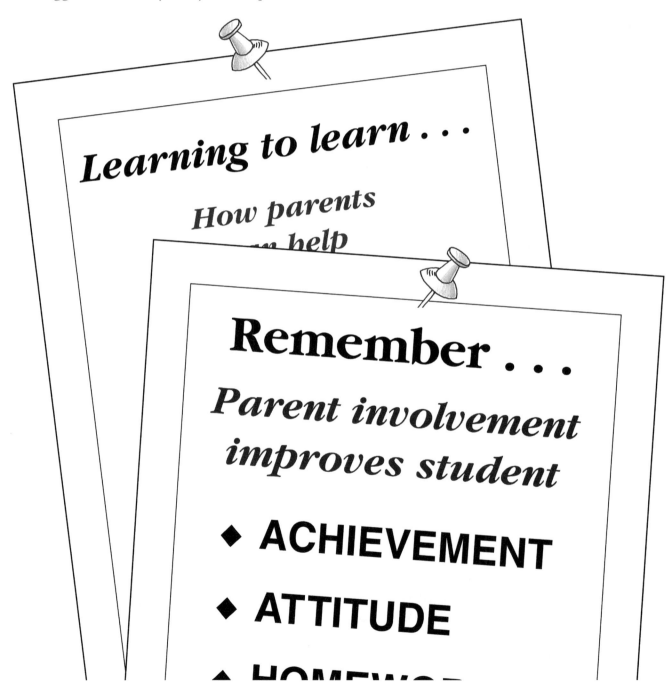

Learning to learn...

How parents
~~n~~ help

Remember . . .

Parent involvement improves student

◆ **ACHIEVEMENT**

◆ **ATTITUDE**

◆ HOMEWO~~R~~

Remember . . .

Parent involvement improves student

- ◆ **ACHIEVEMENT**

- ◆ **ATTITUDE**

- ◆ **HOMEWORK**

- ◆ **GRADES**

- ◆ **ASPIRATIONS**

Learning to learn . . .

How parents can help at home:

◆ **Understand the importance of homework and study time.**

◆ **Take an inventory of basic study skills.**

◆ **Know and apply learning style strategies.**

◆ **Help your child plan and use study time effectively.**

Teaching for Learning Success, Rev. Ed.

HELPFUL STUDY TIME HINTS:
A Practical Guide for Parents

The study hints on the following pages were designed to be copied and sent home to parents (although they are not limited to this purpose, of course). They are intended to introduce parents to positive study strategies so that parents are better able to help the student at home.

Most parents want to help their child at home, but feel inadequate for a number of reasons.

♦ They are not familiar with the concepts and content of a
particular course.

♦ They are afraid of giving incorrect information because they fear
it might have changed since they learned it.

♦ They do not want to share their thinking process because they
fear it will differ from the teacher's explanation and will serve
only to confuse the student.

♦ They do not know where to begin to help.

You can positively affect your students long after they leave your classroom by teaching their parents to provide them with good study tools for years to come. So at every appropriate opportunity, provide parents with these tools by reproducing these pages (as well as any others in this book). You may use these forms in many different ways.

♦ Attach them to parent letters.

♦ Send them home with homework assignments.

♦ Distribute copies at parent-teacher conferences.

♦ Distribute copies during a back-to-school night.

Also consult *Learning to Learn: Strengthening Study Skills and Brain Power, Revised Edition*, by Gloria Frender. Incentive Publications: Nashville, TN, 2004.

Look for a variety of information to add to your "parent" file. Good sources are magazines (professional and other), educational conferences, newspapers, and psychology journals.

PARENT HINT ONE

Institute a regularly scheduled study time every weekday.

STEP 1 ☞ Compute the amount of time your student needs each day for his or her study block:

- ◆ Set study time by using the rule of 10 minutes per grade level, per day, five days a week
  Example: Grade 8 = 80 total minutes of study time each day

- ◆ Set study block time within the study time to make the best use of focused attention span/learning time per grade level by using this guideline:

  - • Primary grades: 10–15 minute study block

  - • Upper elementary: 20 minute study block

  - • Middle/high school: 25–35 minute study block

  - • College/adult: 45 minute study block

- ◆ Set break time to "recharge your brain" by using this guideline:

  - • Primary grades: study 15/ break 10/ study 15 (Gr. 3 example)

  - • Upper elementary: study 20/break 10/study 20/break 10/study 10 (Gr. 5 example)

  - • Middle/high school: study 30/break 10/study 30/break 10/study 30 (Gr. 9 example)

STEP 2 ☞ Use the "Daily Schedule" chart on page 200 to help you find the best time to study. Use one color of ink to write activities in the rectangles. Use horizontal or vertical lines to indicate repeated activities or ones that take up more than one block. Use one color to block out time for:

- ◆ Getting up

- ◆ School (include transportation/walking time to and from school)

- ◆ Eating dinner

- ◆ Going to bed

STEP 3 ☞ Use a second color to block out time for any regular, weekly commitments:
Examples: music lessons, religious activities, sports, club meetings,
family/friends activities

STEP 4 ☞ Use a third color to block out time for:

- ◆ Study time (remember to consider your best focused learning time when you are personally your most productive).

- ◆ Include your break time in addition to your appropriate study time.

- ◆ Use five rectangle blocks that touch by the corners or sides to avoid scattered study time (you cannot make studying a habit this way).

- ◆ Do not begin your study time later than 9:00 pm even if you are a "night person."

Consider these successful pointers.

- • Stick to your schedule for at least one week, then change it if necessary.

- • Don't be afraid to change things around to be more productive.

- • Be flexible, but change something only if there is a good reason.

- • Include some free time each day.

- • Leave some time open for the unexpected.

- • Become familiar with your schedule and make the schedule a habit.

- • Post it and carry it with you so you can easily see it.

	SUN	MON	TUE	WED	THURS	FRI	SAT
2:00				School			
3:00		3:30					
4:00	Study Time	Study Time	Piano Lesson	Study Time	Study Time		
5:00			Study Time		Basketball Practice		
6:00				Dinner			
7:00						Swimming	
8:00		TV					
9:00							
9:30	Bed						

From *Learning To Learn, Rev. Ed.* by Gloria Frender. Nashville, TN: Incentive Publications, ©2004. Used by permission.

DAILY SCHEDULE

	SUN	MON	TUE	WED	THURS	FRI	SAT
5:00							
6:00							
7:00							
8:00							
9:00							
10:00							
11:00							
12:00							
1:00							
2:00							
3:00							
4:00							
5:00							
6:00							
7:00							
8:00							
9:00							
10:00							
11:00							
12:00							

From *Learning To Learn, Rev. Ed.* by Gloria Frender.
Nashville, TN: Incentive Publications, ©2004. Used by permission.

Teaching for Learning Success, Rev. Ed.

PARENT HINT TWO

Find or make the best place to study.

1. The best place to study is away from all distractions. Avoid studying:
   - with the television on
   - with music on
   - when eating
   - near a telephone
   - when sitting or lying on a bed
   - near high-traffic areas

2. Make it a habit to study at the same place and time.

3. Ensure good lighting and ventilation in your study area.

Get organized!

1. Record assignments in an assignment notebook and on a calendar.

2. Supply standard study materials within easy reach of the study area.

3. Ask to see your child's assignment notebook, class calendar, class materials, and textbooks on a regular basis.

4. Find a moment to pleasantly discuss with your child his or her progress in every class.

5. Use "to do" lists on a daily basis to help set priorities.

6. Suggest that your child make a checklist of materials to take home each day.

   Tape or staple the list inside his or her notebook of the last class of the day.

7. Help your child organize notebooks and binders for each class.

   Check periodically to see if your child is maintaining them in an organized manner.

For additional information on study and organizational tips, refer to *Learning to Learn, Revised Edition* by Gloria Frender; Incentive Publications, Inc., Nashville, Tennessee, 2004.

PARENT HINT THREE

Make learning an important and meaningful priority, and help your student understand that he or she must be responsible for his or her learning.

1. Discuss and model your commitment to education. Do your own reading and studying when it is your student's study time.

2. Stress learning strategies as life-long skills.

3. Underscore the importance of reading and writing skills in all curriculum areas, not simply in language arts or literature courses.

4. Limit the use of the television, telephone, music, and other distractions.

5. Give gifts that reinforce good study habits or interests.
   - Give magazine or book subscriptions according to the student's grade level and interests.
   - Give a dictionary, thesaurus, writer's handbook, calculator, colored pens/pencils, desk set, paper organizer, calendar, study lamp, software, etc.

6. Discuss acceptable goals and ways of measuring completion.

   Reward your child when he or she has completed them.

7. Expose your student to various educational opportunities.
   - Visit museums, theater performances, lectures, exhibits, conventions, etc.
   - Be a host family for foreign students.
   - Join clubs or associations that fit your child's needs and interests.
   - Find a mentor to help your child pursue a particular passion.

8. Become involved with your student's school.
   - Join parent support groups.
   - Volunteer in the classroom. Discuss this with your child first to find out how he or she feels about having you present in the classroom. If your child would rather you not volunteer in his or her classroom, volunteer in another one.
   - Be active on parent-teacher committees.
   - Volunteer to type, phone, or assemble packets at home, help in the nurse's office or production room, or help produce the school's parent newsletter.

9. Make contact with teachers on a regular basis.

   ◆ Request a progress report periodically, if needed.

   ◆ Talk with teachers or counselors as a means of "preventive medicine".

10. Find ways to reward positive teaching.

   ◆ Write a thank-you note.

   ◆ Give gift certificates to a favorite bookstore, restaurant, etc.

11. Understand and support teachers' classroom rules. Keep a copy of each teacher's rules on-hand.

12. Be clear and consistent with your expectations.

13. Consistently and fairly apply your rules every day.

14. Openly discuss your values concerning education, and realistically apply them to everyday life. Discuss your child's future and the impact education can have on it.

15. Sincerely listen to any concerns, excuses, and ideas your child shares with you regarding:

   ◆ school   ◆ school administrators

   ◆ classes   ◆ home study time

   ◆ teachers

16. When necessary, take immediate action if your child demonstrates sudden changes in personality, friends, personal habits, etc. Take your child's feelings seriously.

PARENT HINT FOUR

Be a consultant for homework.

1. Provide the right environment for homework and study time and insist that your child uses it.

2. Set specific time limits on your availability during his or her study time.

   If appropriate, arrange to meet with one another every hour or half hour for a progress check during break time.

3. Be positive in actions and words.

4. Be willing to help and guide, but do not give answers or work problems.

   ◆ Ask your child what he or she already knows about the subject.

   ◆ Ask your child how he or she has already tried to solve the problem or learn the information.

   ◆ Direct your child to verbalize why he or she thinks a solution is not available.

   ◆ Provide a variety of ways for your child to complete the task.

   ◆ Watch your child begin to work on the solution, and then encourage independent work.

5. Ask questions that promote higher-level thinking when quizzing your child on materials.

   ◆ "Can you briefly summarize what you just read? What/who was important and why?"

   ◆ "Can you explain your answer?"

   ◆ "Can you state examples and tell why they are important?"

   ◆ "Do you agree? Why or why not?"

   ◆ "How did you arrive at your answer or solution? What were your 'thinking' steps?"

◆ "What facts support your view and can you think of others not stated?"

◆ "Can you apply these ideas to other situations or information?"

◆ "Can you add information to this subject or compare and contrast it with what you already know?"

6. Check to make sure the homework completed matches the assignment.

7. When your child becomes frustrated, show him or her a way to address the problem.

◆ Have your child read the assignment aloud to you, and then discuss it.

◆ Check with your child to see if he or she is using the correct materials to complete the assignment. Ask him or her, "Where else can you look? What other references are available?"

◆ Determine if the problem or assignment has been copied correctly. Has your child checked his or her work?

◆ Tell your child to call a classmate for clarification or additional information if necessary.

◆ Tell your child to write out the material or assignment, draw it as a picture, make a chart or graph of the information, etc.

◆ Ask your child to look at the process being used to learn the information or solve the problem. Should the approach be changed?

◆ Try to connect the information with something he or she already knows about the subject.

◆ Ask your child what he or she thinks the teacher would say, do, or ask.

◆ Divide the assignment or problem into smaller parts.

◆ Instruct him or her to use all senses to solve the problem. Hear it, see it, say it, write it, and do it.

◆ Help him or her understand why the information is important and how it can be applied in the future.

PARENT HINT FIVE

Plan Ahead.

USE A MONTHLY CALENDAR

Using a monthly calendar helps students to make a commitment to planning ahead. It also helps everyone to see the whole picture of many weeks at one time and physically shows sequential steps necessary to complete a project/assignment on time. Help your student with the following exercise.

- With a full piece of poster board:
  - Use a wide, black felt marker and yardstick to mark off squares large enough to include several written activities/tasks.
  - Include all seven days of the week and a total of five weeks. At the top of each column, label the days of the week, leaving a blank space for the month name.
  - Cover the entire calendar with dull, translucent contact paper, or buy large, laminated, one- and two-month calendars from office supply stores.
  - Use a black water-soluble transparency pen to fill in the correct numbered days and the name of the month.
  - Use colored water-soluble transparency pens to write in all assignments. Match each color with the appropriate subject—the same ones your student uses for his or her notebooks .
- Use two (or even three) calendars when assignments are spread over several weeks or months.
- Place the calendar(s) on a wall or bulletin board in the student's room where it is easily seen and accessible.
- Use a damp paper towel to clean the calendar off for the next month.

BREAK DOWN LONG-TERM ASSIGNMENTS

The process of breaking down long-term assignments into smaller units helps the left and right brain work together to organize specific steps that result in a completed project. Auditory, visual, and kinesthetic learners will benefit greatly by talking aloud while writing and reviewing the specific steps as needed. Help lower everyone's stress level and raise your student's success level by following these steps .

1. Use the correct color of pen for each subject throughout this process.

2. Write in the date the assignment was given.
   Example: May 1, Science Report Assigned

3. Write in the date the assignment is due by using "Report Really Due." Then in the

day before write, "Report Due" which is really Final Draft: Second Edit. Always allow one extra day to correct anything that may go wrong at the last minute. Plus, it leaves one extra day to relax and not panic. *Example:* May 30, Science Report Due (teacher's date is actually May 31)

4. Count the number of days between the assignment date and the "Report Due" date; divide that number into fourths, halves and three-fourths. Write "$^1/_4$", "$^1/_2$", and "$^3/_4$" on the appropriate dates.

5. Next, write three steps that should be completed for each date. For example:
   - On May 7: $^1/_4$ Sci. Rep.: topic narrowed, references checked out, double-check assignment
   - On May 15: $^1/_2$ Sci. Rep.: research completed, note cards organized, begin rough draft
   - On May 22: $^3/_4$ Sci. Rep.: first draft completed, edit final outline, begin works cited
   - Review dates for accuracy, conflicts, and assignments. Make adjustments as required. (For example, if there is a busy test schedule on May 15, move the $^1/_2$ to May 14 or May 16).

6. Work backwards from the "Report Due" date (May 30) to schedule 24 hours of not working on the assignment (see *"Hint for Written Assignments"* below). Schedule a "Final Draft: First Edit" and a "Final Draft: Second Edit."

7. Post a copy of the calendar in a place it will be seen every day as a reminder.

8. STICK TO THE SCHEDULE!

Hint:
FOR WRITTEN ASSIGNMENTS

Always leave 24 hours between the time the final edited draft is finished and the final read-through before turning it in. This allows the student's brain to refocus on other things so upon rereading the final draft he or she will catch mistakes that were not apparent on previous editing.

Hint:
FOR READING ASSIGNMENTS

Break down the reading by writing specific pages to be read each day (Mon. pp 1–15, Tues. pp 16–30, etc.) Remember to leave enough time to write the report, too.

     From *Learning To Learn, Rev. Ed.* by Gloria Frender. Nashville, TN: Incentive Publications, ©2004. Used by permission.

PARENT HINT SIX

Create daily "to do" lists.

This activity takes about 10 minutes to complete, yet it saves many hours of work and prevents a great deal of frustration.

1. Sit down with your child and discuss why it is important to make a daily list of things to do. Remind him or her that people are ten times more likely to do something if they write it down. Share a personal experience that illustrates the truth of this statement.

2. Have your child write on the "to do" list three tasks to be accomplished the next day in both the "need to do" and "want to do" columns. (Work only one day at a time.) Explain that these tasks cannot be trivial or unrealistic. For example, going to school, coming home from school, and eating are trivial activities, and going to Disneyland, staying up all night, and spending the day at the mall are unrealistic activities for a school day.

3. Have your student label each item with an M, A, or N (morning, afternoon, or night activity).

4. Have your child combine the tasks in both columns into one list. Again, stress making a schedule that is fair and realistic. Choose a task form the "need" column first, then reward it with an item from the "want" list, if possible.

5. Review the final "to do" list. Ask your child if the list is realistic.

6. If one task from the final list does not get completed, add it to the next day's "to do" list, if this is possible.

CREATING A "TO DO" LIST

Need To Do	Want To Do	Final "To Do" List
		1.
		2.
		3.
		4.
		5.
		6.
		7.
		8.

Need To Do	Want To Do	Final "To Do" List
		1.
		2.
		3.
		4.
		5.
		6.
		7.
		8.

Use 3" x 5" index cards for future "to do" lists. Remember, it takes doing something 14 days in a row in the same place and at the same time to form a habit. Create a "to do" list for the following day each night before you go to bed.

PARENT GUIDELINES:
—— Helping Frustrated Students at Home ——

When your child comes to you for help because he or she is frustrated in class, try these strategies. Don't feel intimidated if you are not familiar with the course content. You can still help your child to learn. Ask your child the following questions in this order:

1. "What do you already know about this topic or subject?"

2. "Why is this important information to learn? How can you use this in the future?"

3. "How have you tried to learn this already? What do you need to change to learn this?"

4. "How can you divide this material into smaller units for easier learning? How can you divide this material into some main topic areas, then link the details to each topic?"

5. "Show me a system or strategy you have for learning this material." (for example, a graphic organizer, mnemonic device, etc.)

 Teaching for Learning Success, Rev. Ed.

PARENT-TEACHER CONFERENCES

MATERIALS

- notebook
- pens
- blank paper and extra pens (for parental use)
- parent-teacher conference schedule (Be sure to write in student's name if it differs from parent's name.)
- gradebook
- copy of midterm grades, discipline letters (refer to pages 124–129), and any other important papers
- a sign (if necessary) with your room number and name posted on the outside of your classroom door
- two chairs placed outside your door on which parents may sit if they must wait
- one copy of class textbook within easy reach
- one copy of every monthly newsletter
- copies of student assignments for that class
- copies of the parent letter (refer to page 214)

TWO WEEKS BEFORE THE CONFERENCES

Review school policy regarding students attending parent-teacher conferences. If there is no formal policy on this matter, make a decision about their attendance and let the students know well ahead of time if they are expected to attend. Include this information in your monthly newsletter, or add it to your parent letter concerning conferences (see page 214).

GETTING ORGANIZED

1. Arrange student desks or chairs in a circle around a table to provide for better communication.

2. Arrange student folders, packets, and other materials in order of the scheduled conferences; place a colored sheet of paper between each student's papers for quick retrieval.

3. Bring your gradebook, scan sheets, progress records, and student portfolios for quick reference. You may want to make several copies of your gradebook or scan sheet if you plan to show parents their own child's grades but do not wish them to see other students' grades.

PARENT-TEACHER CONFERENCES

4. Place the conference schedule in a location where you can refer to it frequently.

5. Carefully review parents' and student's names if they are not the same.

6. Review student folders quickly to be sure that everything you require is in them, as well as to reacquaint yourself with each student's work.

7. Copy helpful, informative study skills handouts to give to parents so that they may better help the student at home.

8. Try to stay on schedule. Make another conference appointment or set up a time to call to discuss any unfinished business.

THE CONFERENCE

1. Greet parent(s) with a handshake.

2. Begin the conference with a positive statement about their child and acknowledge any areas of improvement, accomplishment, or effort.

3. State simply and directly the student's progress as you observe it in the following areas:

   ◆ adjustment to the grade level, new school, new situation, etc.

   ◆ emotional development; maturity level appropriate to grade level

   ◆ social development, peer relationships, interacting with persons in authority, and general classroom behavior

   ◆ academic performance (class participation, completion of assignments on time, quality and pride in work, working to ability, performing below, at, or above grade level, observable study habits and self-initiative, ownership of learning)

4. Clarify any areas in need of improvement.

5. Offer suggestions and/or materials to remediate areas of need. Elicit responses and ideas from parent(s) and decide on a plan of remediation. Be sure you both agree on the plan—the student will benefit most from home and school working together.

6. Write down any plans and goals (be specific) in your notebook for your future reference; be sure the parent(s) do the same.

7. If needed, set specific dates for further contact.

8. Review any plans for future action.

9. Ask parent(s) if they have any further questions or concerns.

10. Tell them to feel free to call you at any time.

11. Make any necessary copies of student contracts, etc. for parents to take with them.

12. Walk them to the classroom door, and shake hands.

SUGGESTIONS

Always include the principal or any other administrator or counselor in a parent-teacher conference when you feel their input will be a positive addition or further support to you.

If students are included in the conferences, have them write down any plans for alleviating areas of concern and repeat them back to you; be sure they have a clear understanding of everything mentioned in the conference. Be positive, too!

Date: _____

Dear Parents,

Parent-teacher conferences will be held soon. This is an opportunity for us to discuss your student's progress.

I encourage you to prepare for the conference by reading through and thinking about the following suggestions. Please respond by jotting down any questions or thoughts you might have and bringing them with you to the conference.

1. Make a list of anything you want to discuss.

   _____

   _____

   _____

2. Ask your child if there is anything he or she wants to include.

   _____

   _____

   _____

3. Ask yourself, "Is my child . . . ?"
   - working to his or her potential and ability
   - functioning below, at, or above grade level
   - coming to class prepared
   - demonstrating appropriate classroom behavior
   - respectful
   - using good study skills and work habits
   - making appropriate progress
   - getting along well with peers

4. At home, do you observe any specific problems related to school?

   _____

   _____

   _____

Thank you for your time and consideration in preparing for the conference. I look forward to meeting with you.

Sincerely,

CROSS-CONTENT
SKILLS AND MATERIALS

     ✍ *Indicates ready-to-use forms or handouts*

CROSS-CONTENT
SKILLS AND MATERIALS:
An Overview

Teaching learning skills that all students can apply in any content area is every teacher's responsibility.

If you teach students how to learn when presenting the material in your content area, they will have the skills to retain and apply that information. Teaching them how to learn also supplies them with all of the tools they will need for independent learning the rest of their lives.

The materials contained in this section cover a wide variety of topics and needs. You might want to skim each page before you decide if you will be able to use it, keeping in mind your specific classroom goals. The reproducible handouts may be duplicated for distribution to an entire class or to individual students, used as overhead transparencies to reinforce or introduce a concept or class discussion, or posted on bulletin boards. Think of ways to combine each learning strategy with a specific concept or homework assignment.

Remember, teaching students how to learn as well as what to learn makes every student more successful.

CLASS SUMMARY LOG

Do you ever wish your students would take time before leaving class to think for a few moments about some of the major concepts you just taught them? Most students will not do this on their own, but can be trained to summarize class material under your tutelage. One method of introducing students to the concept of summarizing is the use of class summary logs. Summary logs are wonderful learning tools that allow students an accessible format for reviewing important class concepts. They are also easy to administer, producing positive results with little effort.

A class summary log is composed of an oral summary of important class concepts by either you or your students and a written summary of the lesson by each student. These summaries can be completed during the final minutes of class. The combination of an oral review followed by the active learning process of writing a summary successfully reinforces material while helping students retain and transfer information.

For the amount of effort invested, this activity yields high dividends. Because your time (and your students' time) is valuable, invest it wisely. The following pages explain in detail the basic procedure for administering class summary logs. As always, feel free to make any modifications to better suit your teaching style.

WHAT

- ◆ A class summary log is a collection of brief daily entries for each class consisting of
2-3 concepts, new vocabulary words, ideas or questions, etc.

- ◆ Each student writes a log entry during the last few minutes of class.

WHY

- ◆ Class summary logs encourage focused attention in class.

- ◆ The use of summary logs forces students to summarize major concepts on a daily basis.

- ◆ The use of summary logs encourages students to think of appropriate questions related to concepts being studied.

- ◆ Class summary logs reinforce good study skills (and hopefully encourage students to form good study habits).

- ◆ They show the student that he or she did learn something.

- ◆ They provide a source of reference when studying for tests, quizzes, etc., and when completing homework assignments.

- ◆ They require students to review classroom vocabulary words.

MATERIALS

- ◆ loose-leaf paper in a binder or separate notebook (for students)

- ◆ pen or pencil (for students)

- ◆ 2–3 minutes at the end of class

HOW

1. Tell students that they are required to set aside a section of their binders or notebooks for an ongoing summary log; encourage them to use plastic tabs for easy location of their summary logs.

2. Discuss the benefits of this simple activity.

3. Make a transparency of the sample summary log found on page 221 and review some of the examples.

CLASS SUMMARY LOG

4. Make your expectations very clear. Their summaries should include:

- new vocabulary words

- important phrases

- questions students want to ask during the next day's class or look up later

- background information or questions

- thoughts on how they might apply this information in the future

- simple "mind maps" that demonstrate overlapping or connecting information

- concepts particularly stressed by the teacher

- notes to themselves regarding specific worksheets, textbook pages, handouts of particular importance, etc.

5. Allow 2–3 minutes at the end of every class during which students write entries in their logs. This should be an independent activity carried out quietly.

6. All entries should be dated.

7. Many entries may be placed on one page.

8. Except for new vocabulary words or other information you have stressed for correct spelling or exact wording, spelling and complete sentences should not matter. The idea is to get the information on paper.

9. Occasionally review students' entries for completion and quality.

SUGGESTIONS

Periodically collect logs to indicate their importance to students. Consider some type of grade, extra credit points, reward, etc., for acceptable logs.

To stress the importance of quality logs, give a pop quiz and let the students use their logs to answer the questions. This demonstrates to students the type of information you think they should be writing in their logs and gives everyone a chance to do well on a quiz.

SAMPLE SUMMARY LOG

Janie Nose

9/13 Baleen whales   text p. 47 - identification
  • humpback   chart
  • fin
  • blue

9/14 Migration patterns
Gestation period
Orca
  • killer whale
  • largest member of dolphin family
pods
dolphins (sub-family of whales)

9/15 Stressed types of whales
coloration patterns important
— see handout #23

9/16
```
              WHALES
            /        \
       baleen        toothed
          |        eat larger prey
      strainers    not as large as baleen
      no teeth
```

STUDENT RESPONSE SHEET:
—————— Tracking Class Participation ——————

It is a good idea to keep a formal record of individual student participation during class discussions, especially if you plan to assign a participation grade for the course. The form on the following page provides a simple method for keeping track of those students who make an effort to participate in class discussions and those who do not.

You may either maintain the record yourself during class discussions or assign the task to a student. If you decide to allow a student to complete the form, assign an amount of points to be given to that student as he or she will not be able to participate in the discussion that day. Allowing a student to maintain the form frees you to concentrate on the discussion; however, if student participation represents a crucial part of the grade or the discussion is entirely student driven, you may want to score the discussion yourself.

Complete the grade key in the upper right-hand corner of the form with your system for scoring. (For example, "One check or dash equals one point.") Use the space directly below the days of the week to write in specific dates, if necessary.

Teaching for Learning Success, Rev. Ed.

STUDENT RESPONSE SHEET

(Class Participation)

Class _____ Topic _____

Period _____ Date(s) _____

Grade Key:

Student Name	Monday	Tuesday	Wednesday	Thursday	Friday

STUDY TIME WARM-UP

The following handout was designed to accompany a home-work assignment given early in the course. It will help your students more efficiently review the information you covered in class and summarize the main points before actually beginning the assignment. Each time this type of quick review takes place, it increases students' long-term memory and comprehension. It also helps students see the information as a whole and greatly aids their ability to recall details.

Suggestion

Begin every class with a short review of the previous class's main concepts, vocabulary words, etc. Research indicates that a summary at the end of class also helps students remember infor-mation more easily and for a longer period of time.

STUDY TIME WARM-UP

Your mind operates much better when it is warmed up and ready to go. It is similar to starting up a car on a cold day. You have to put the key in the ignition, turn on the engine, and let the engine run for a little while to warm it up. Then, when you want to go somewhere, the whole car will run smoothly and efficiently!

Think of this analogy the next time you sit down to study. Here is a simple checklist to follow to help you focus your mind and warm it up so that you can make the very best use of your study time.

Warm up your mind every time you begin to study! Link the following questions and answers with physical actions:

Physical Action	Question	Answer
1. Pull your chair out from your desk. →	1. What should I study first? →	1. Geometry
2. Sit down in your chair. →	2. What did we do in class today? What was the topic? →	2. Types of triangles
3. Open your book or notebook. Pick up your pencil. →	3. What are three specific concepts or new vocabulary words? →	3. Right triangle, obtuse triangle, acute triangle

Memory Tip

When trying to form a habit with anything that must be done in a sequence, link the ideas with familiar sequential physical actions.

ATTACKING AN ASSIGNMENT

The handout on the following page was designed to accompany the students' first assignment home. Encourage students to share these tips with their parents. You might want to take a few minutes to fully explain the exercise to your students. Relate a personal experience you had when using this step-by-step approach. Mention to them that the process may seem a little time consuming at first, but, as it becomes a habit, it will save them a great deal of time and frustration.

This is a great handout for back-to-school nights and parent-teacher conferences!

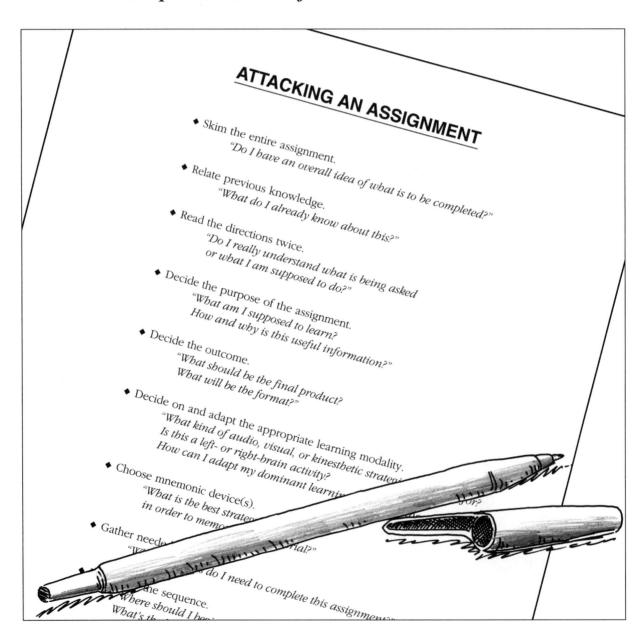

ATTACKING AN ASSIGNMENT

♦ Skim the entire assignment.
"Do I have an overall idea of what is to be completed?"

♦ Relate previous knowledge.
"What do I already know about this?"

♦ Read the directions twice.
"Do I really understand what is being asked or what I am supposed to do?"

♦ Decide the purpose of the assignment.
"What am I supposed to learn?
How and why is this useful information?"

♦ Decide the outcome.
"What should be the final product?
What will be the format?"

♦ Decide on and adapt the appropriate learning modality.
"What kind of audio, visual, or kinesthetic strateg...
Is this a left- or right-brain activity?
How can I adapt my dominant learni...

♦ Choose mnemonic device(s).
"What is the best strate...
in order to memo...

♦ Gather need...
"...al?"
...do I need to complete this assignment...

...he sequence.
Where should I beg...
What's th...

ATTACKING AN ASSIGNMENT

◆ Skim the entire assignment.
> *"Do I have an overall idea of what is to be completed?"*

◆ Relate previous knowledge.
> *"What do I already know about this?"*

◆ Read the directions twice.
> *"Do I really understand what is being asked*
> *or what I am supposed to do?"*

◆ Decide the purpose of the assignment.
> *"What am I supposed to learn?*
> *How and why is this useful information?"*

◆ Decide the outcome.
> *"What should be the final product?*
> *What will be the format?"*

◆ Decide on and adapt the appropriate learning modality.
> *"What kind of audio, visual, or kinesthetic strategies are asked for?*
> *Is this a left- or right-brain activity?*
> *How can I adapt my dominant learning strategy to the assignment?"*

◆ Choose mnemonic device(s).
> *"What is the best strategy to apply*
> *in order to memorize this material?"*

◆ Gather needed materials.
> *"What materials do I need to complete this assignment?"*

◆ Determine the sequence.
> *"Where should I begin?*
> *What's the best sequence?"*

◆ Do the assignment.
> *"Do I intend to learn this information?"*

◆ Review.
> *"Could I teach this to someone else?"*

SUPER NOTE-TAKING SYSTEM

The note-taking system discussed on the following pages is a highly effective and efficient system for both text and class note-taking. The first time you ask students to read a portion of their textbook for homework, introduce to them this note-taking system. Tell them to read the assignment for understanding, and bring their notes back to class to use as a listening guide.

1. Use the information found on page 229 as an aid for introducing the "Super Note-taking System". Have students make three columns on a sheet of their notebook paper and label each column.

2. Thoroughly explain to students how to use the note-taking system, and discuss any questions students may have.

3. Use the sample note-taking form on page 230 as a transparency to show students how notes from a science text and lecture might look.

4. Using the information sheet and sample note-taking form, discuss the upcoming assignment. If needed, complete the first section of the handout in class, using the first paragraph from their reading assignment.

5. At the beginning of class the following day, display a sample transparency that you made from the reading assignment, and review how their notes might look.

Suggestion

Note how the main topics, subtopics, and details are arranged on the sample form. The mind retrieves information more quickly and retains it better when it is written in a simple format. Encourage students to write only key words, and then indent and use a bullet or dash to set off details. Leave spaces between major concepts. Share this information with students when introducing note taking.

Teaching for Learning Success, Rev. Ed.

WHY

◆ This system saves students time by providing a format that combines text and class notes with important vocabulary words.

◆ It provides a "ready-made" study sheet that helps students quiz themselves before tests.

◆ It saves students time in class by eliminating the need to rewrite lecture notes that repeat the same information as that of the text notes.

◆ It helps students organize lecture notes in an orderly manner, thereby reducing stress in class.

WHEN

◆ Whenever possible, students should take text notes before attending class. This gives them more time to organize their thoughts into a system according to main topics.

◆ Students should take text notes to class to add any new information that the teacher provides. Lecture information that repeats text notes can be underlined, highlighted, or checked off.

HOW

◆ Ask students to carefully examine the sample handout and notice the organizational pattern of the concepts and the details. Single words and simple phrases are used—complex or complete sentences are not. Also, point out the use of spaces and indentations to help the mind organize information and remember it longer. Page numbers are written in the "Key Words" column to save time if students need to refer to the text for further information.

◆ Students take notes from the reading assignment on the blank form, referring to the example as often as necessary.

◆ A key word is written in the left column. Notes related to that key word are written in the middle column marked "Text Notes." Spaces are left between concepts to add additional lecture notes if needed.

◆ The Vocabulary Abbreviation Key at the top of the page contains abbreviations of key words used in the lecture. This will enable students to write faster and later understand the abbreviated words.

◆ Make flash cards out of the key words.

$\mathcal{S}$AMPLE: NOTE-TAKING FORM

Vocabulary Abbreviation Key

C—Cetacea

BW—baleen whales

H—humpbacks

Class **Science**

Date **9/27**

Name **Rachelle Blair**

Oceanography Unit

Key Word	Text Notes	Class Notes
Cetacea 44	*Cetacea (whales)*	

baleen 45	*Baleen whales (main topic)*
	• *use baleens: (sub topic)*
	  no teeth (detail)
	    • *feather-like*
	    • *strain plankton*
	• *size:*
	    • *20'–100'*
	• *travel in pods*
	    • *5–30 whales*
	    • *male leader*
	• *three types:*
	    • *humpback (example)*
	    • *blue*
	    • *fin*
		• *pleated throat*
		    • *gulp in water*
		    • *push back thru baleen*
		        • *capture plankton*
		• *hunted for:*
		    • *meat*
		    • *oil (blubber)*
		    • *bone*

humpback 46	*humpbacks*
	• *known for: songs/males*
	• *size:*
	    • *62'*
	    • *53 tons*
		• *coloration: (sub topic)*
		    • *black (detail)*
		        • *except parts/*
		        underside
		        (sub detail)

From *Learning To Learn, Rev. Ed.* by Gloria Frender.
Nashville, TN: Incentive Publications, ©2004. Used by permission.

Teaching for Learning Success, Rev. Ed.

OTE-TAKING FORM

Vocabulary Abbreviation Key

Class _____

Date _____

Name _____

_____

Key Word	Text Notes	Class Notes

SUPER STUDY SHEETS

Students often have trouble studying for tests because they do not know how to effectively use their notes and handouts. To process and comprehend information, students need to become active instead of passive learners. An active learner manipulates and reformats information, while a passive learner simply rereads it. Every time the mind actively uses information, it remembers it longer. The mind also learns more quickly when information is divided into organized topics.

The Super Study Sheets handout on the following page teaches students how to turn passive learning into active learning. Distribute the study sheet instructions (page 233) to students a few days before your first test and review with them the step-by-step procedure, using references specific to the upcoming test. You may want to reproduce and distribute the learning chart on page 234, as well as hang a copy of it on your bulletin board.

If you have not introduced graphic organizers to your students, now is a good time to do so as it is suggested in the following materials to use graphic organizers as a part of the study process. (Refer to the section on graphic organizers, pages 235–247.)

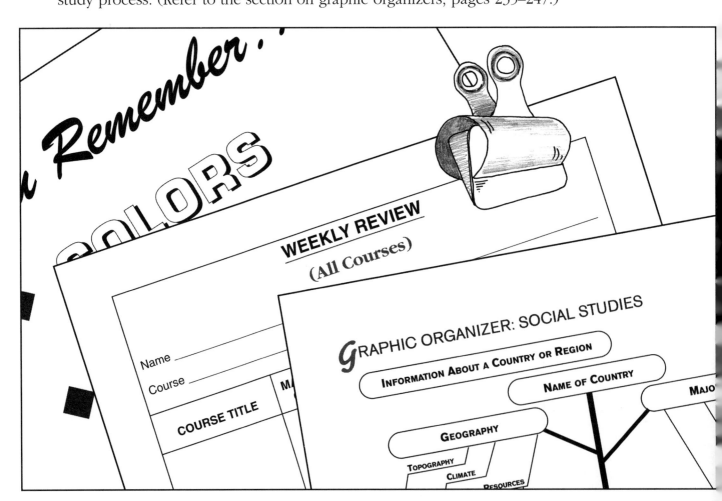

SUPER STUDY SHEETS

WHY

- Super Study Sheets help you organize your notes so that you can learn more effectively.

- They greatly reduce the number of pages you need to study.

- They encourage you to become an active learner by asking you to repeatedly process information in different ways.

- They save you time studying for tests as you do not have to start from the beginning every time you prepare to study.

- They assist you in condensing, simplifying, and learning information faster.

- They make studying less stressful.

WHEN

- Construct study sheets once a week for each subject.

- Combine and review study sheets a few days before a test.

- Review study sheets and graphic organizers often to avoid the need to "cram" for a test.

HOW

- Review the steps of pre-reading the chapter or unit

- Set yourself up for memory and comprehension success by giving your mind a purpose to read. If it has a specific purpose to retain information before you actually begin reading, you probably will not have to reread it—and that saves time!

- Read just one paragraph at a time (without taking notes) for these three categories:
  - Main topic
  - Sub-topic
  - Details and Examples

- Begin taking notes using the steps given in the "Super Note-taking System".

You Remember....

◆ COLORS

◆ SHAPES

◆ PLACEMENT

◆ WORDS

◆ 123456789

GRAPHIC ORGANIZERS

Graphic organizers are highly powerful learning tools designed to incorporate learning strategies that the mind quickly absorbs and easily retains: colors, shapes, and placement.

The following section on graphic organizers contains detailed directions on the construction of graphic organizers, a list of possible uses, instructions on how to use them to improve your teaching to students with varied learning styles, and numerous patterns for organizers (pages 240–247) to be reproduced and used for transparencies and handouts. (Modify them to best suit your particular needs or make up some of your own!)

A graphic organizer:

- helps students focus on concepts and relate what they already know by using colors, shapes, and placement as the focus of a handout's design

- visually illustrates ideas and concepts using written and verbal text

- clearly demonstrates the overall organization of concepts and their details

- increases comprehension and encourages organized thinking

- demonstrates step-by-step procedures and general flow of material

- provides as a listening guide for lectures when used as an overhead transparency

MATERIALS

- unit plan, handouts, other materials

- blank transparencies

- copy machine which makes transparencies from masters

- colored transparency pens

- plastic template with numerous simple shapes (see "Suggestions for Creating Handouts and Tests," pages 92–94)

- transparent tape

- overhead projector

- screen

GRAPHIC ORGANIZERS

WHAT

A graphic organizer (also known as an advanced organizer, mind map, spider web, or listening guide) is a highly powerful teaching and learning tool that presents information in an organized manner using colors, shapes, and placement.

WHY

Graphic organizers are super tools to help you strengthen your brain power. They are very successful because they work with the way you learn and incorporate many positive aspects of what research tells us about learning. Creating graphic organizers the right way brings all your learning modalities together at once to produce a fantastic memory so you can recall facts when you need them. They allow you to use the most powerful learning tools for your brain all at once.

Graphic organizers allow you to:

- see the whole picture/end result and how concepts relate to each other or build on each other (right brain).

- see individual parts/details, how they are broken down to smaller parts, and how they work to make a whole (left brain).

- use colors, shapes, placement, and words/numbers (quick recognition and long-term factors).

- incorporate all the learning modalities (visual, auditory, and kinesthetic).

- HEAR IT—talk out loud to yourself all the time while studying (except when reading for speed).

- SAY IT—be aware of your thoughts as you say it out loud.

- WRITE IT—write the information so your mind will see the words and patterns.

- SEE IT—watch yourself while you write it.

GRAPHIC ORGANIZERS

♦ DO IT—be physically active by reorganizing the information from your notes onto another paper by condensing the information into a pattern.

♦ comprehend and memorize simple and complicated material easily.

♦ learn large amounts of material with greater recall.

♦ recreate these organizers from memory on test papers to greatly reduce stress, combat confusion, and provide direction for essays.

You can see how powerful these study tools can be for your learning. Study the "Sample: Pizza Graphic Organizer" before constructing one of your own.

HOW

♦ Select one main category from your notes and/or handouts.

♦ Write the main topic at the center of your paper using one color of ink (see "Sample: Pizza Graphic Organizer" on page 238).

♦ Take a major sub-topic and write it inside a simple shape off to the side of the main topic (use the color coding on your notes—see sample: meat on pizza).

  • Use one color for the main topic and a different color for each sub-topic shape and detail (do not use shades of the same color, or similar colors such as pink, red, or orange in the same organizer).

  • Example (see "Sample: Pizza Graphic Organizer") Pizza (black ink); the rectangle and words: meat, pepperoni, sausage, Canadian bacon (red ink); the oval and words: green peppers, olive, mushrooms (green ink).

♦ Use straight lines to write in details and connect them to the sub-topic shape (use the color coding on your notes—see example: pepperoni on pizza).

♦ Repeat the previous two steps as many times as needed.

♦ Remember to abbreviate all words.

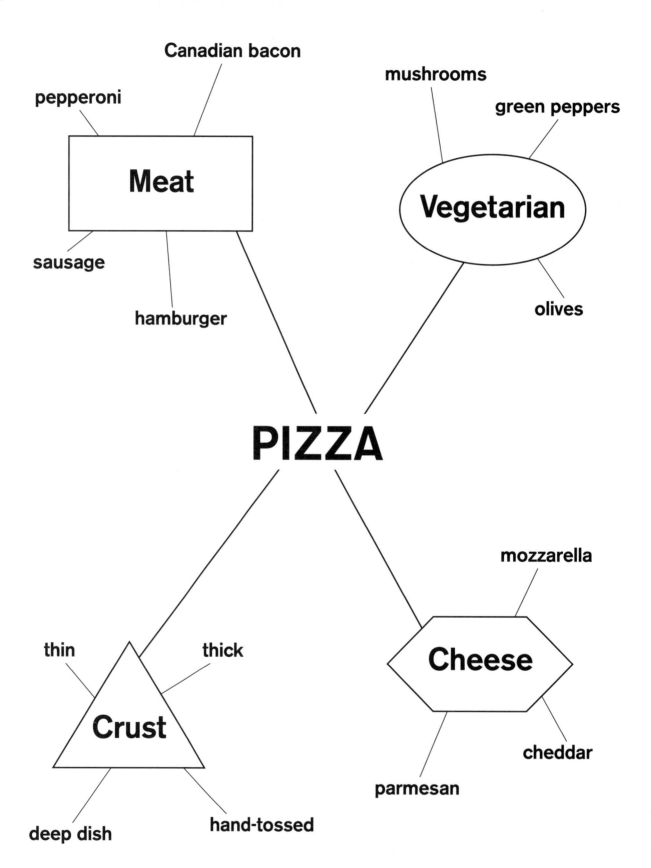

USES FOR GRAPHIC ORGANIZERS

A graphic organizer may be used as a(n):

◆ listening guide for note taking during lectures and films

◆ pretest on new material
(individual, group, or class activity)

◆ introduction of new material

◆ review activity for tests
(student-generated organizer covering main concepts and important details of unit or teacher-generated organizer with shapes/format and one or two words filled in)

◆ brainstorming activity
(for essays, written assignments, group projects and presentations, report overviews)

◆ summarizing activity
(individual, group, or whole-class summaries of text notes, class notes, class discussions, group presentations, etc.)

◆ bulletin board display
(large class graphic organizer displayed on a bulletin board)

◆ organizational planning tool
(an overview for group presentations, class discussions, etc.)

From *Learning To Learn, Rev. Ed.* by Gloria Frender.
Nashville, TN: Incentive Publications, ©2004. Used by permission.

GRAPHIC ORGANIZER: MAIN IDEA – SUPPORTING IDEAS – DETAILS

MAIN IDEA　　　　**SUPPORTING IDEAS**　　　　**DETAILS**

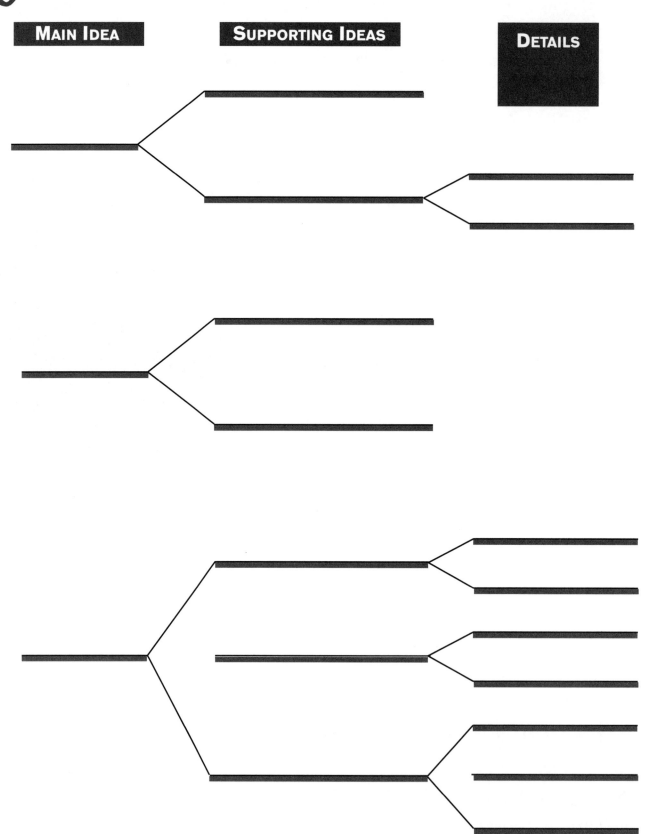

Teaching for Learning Success, Rev. Ed.

GRAPHIC ORGANIZER: MAIN TOPIC – SUBTOPIC – DETAILS AND EXAMPLES

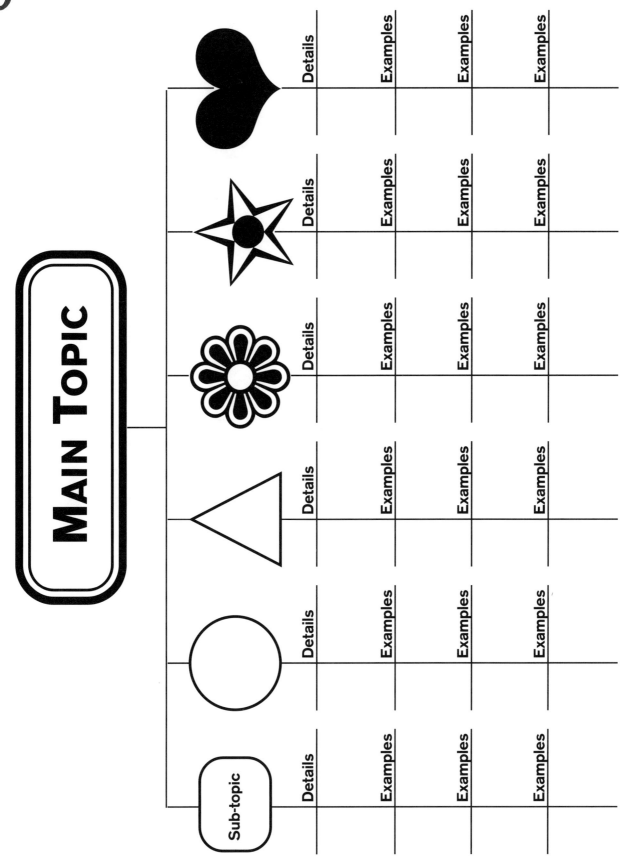

GRAPHIC ORGANIZER: CYCLE

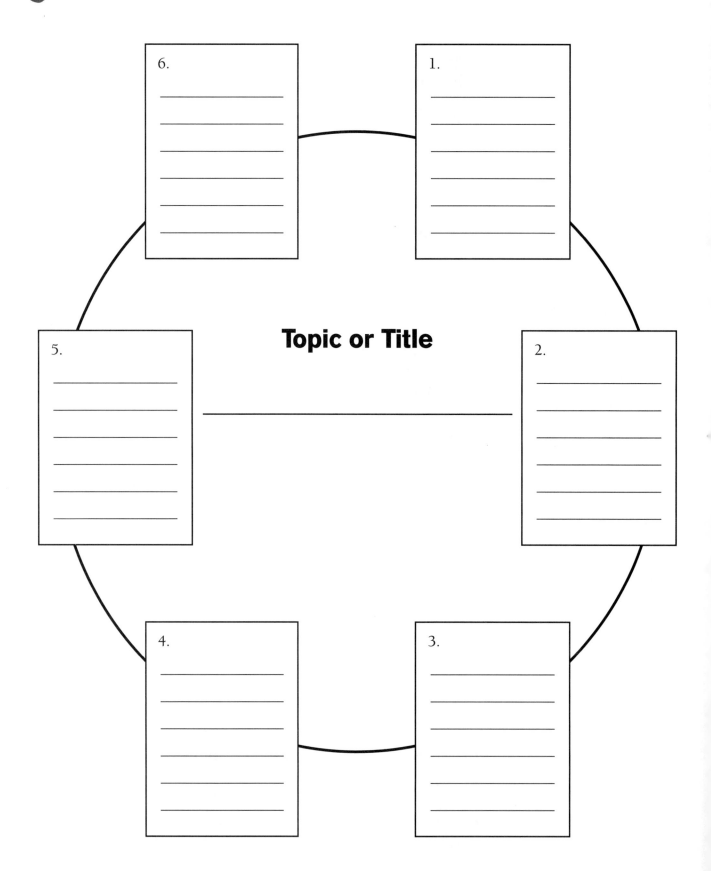

6.

1.

5.

Topic or Title

2.

4.

3.

From *Learning To Learn, Rev. Ed.* by Gloria Frender.
Nashville, TN: Incentive Publications, ©2004. Used by permission.

Teaching for Learning Success, Rev. Ed.

GRAPHIC ORGANIZER: COMMON CHARACTERISTICS

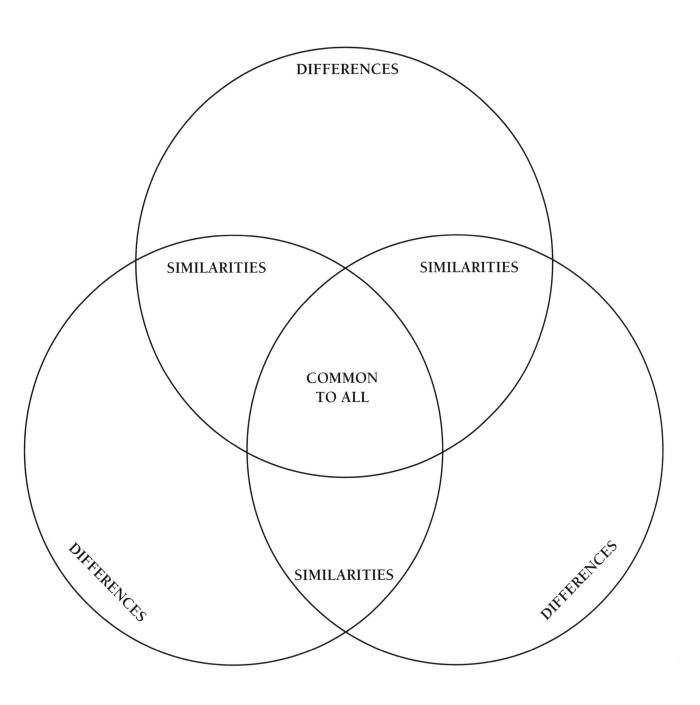

DIFFERENCES

SIMILARITIES

SIMILARITIES

COMMON
TO ALL

DIFFERENCES

SIMILARITIES

DIFFERENCES

From *Learning To Learn, Rev. Ed.* by Gloria Frender.
Nashville, TN: Incentive Publications, ©2004. Used by permission.

*G*RAPHIC ORGANIZER: TIMELINE

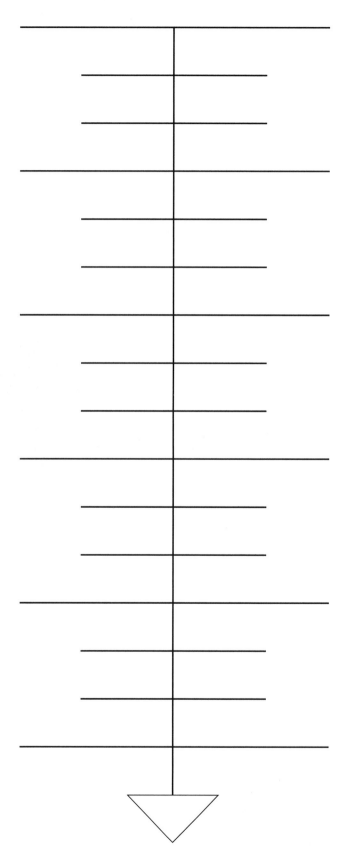

From *Learning To Learn, Rev. Ed.* by Gloria Frender.
Nashville, TN: Incentive Publications, ©2004. Used by permission.

Teaching for Learning Success, Rev. Ed.

$\mathcal{G}$RAPHIC ORGANIZER: TREE

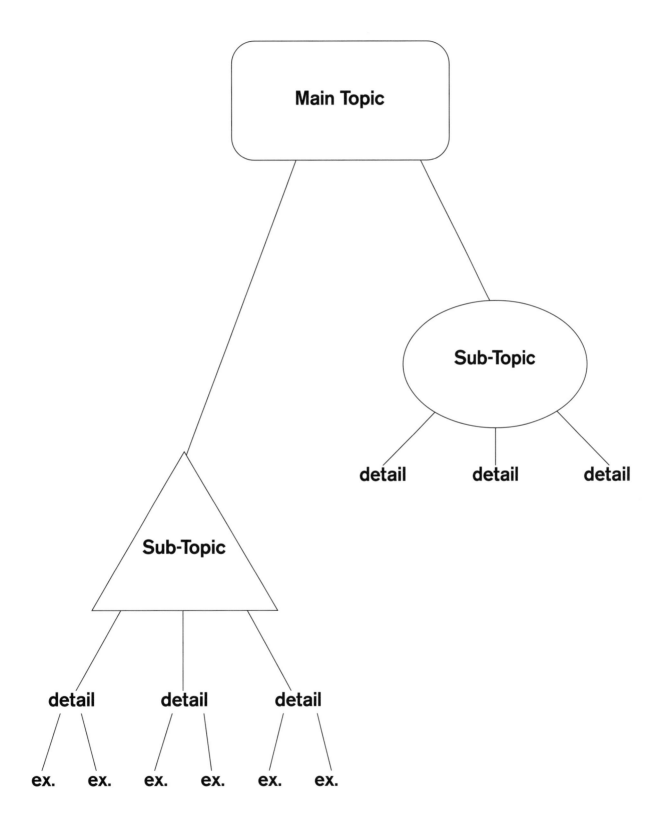

From *Learning To Learn, Rev. Ed.* by Gloria Frender.
Nashville, TN: Incentive Publications, ©2004. Used by permission.

GRAPHIC ORGANIZER: BIOGRAPHY

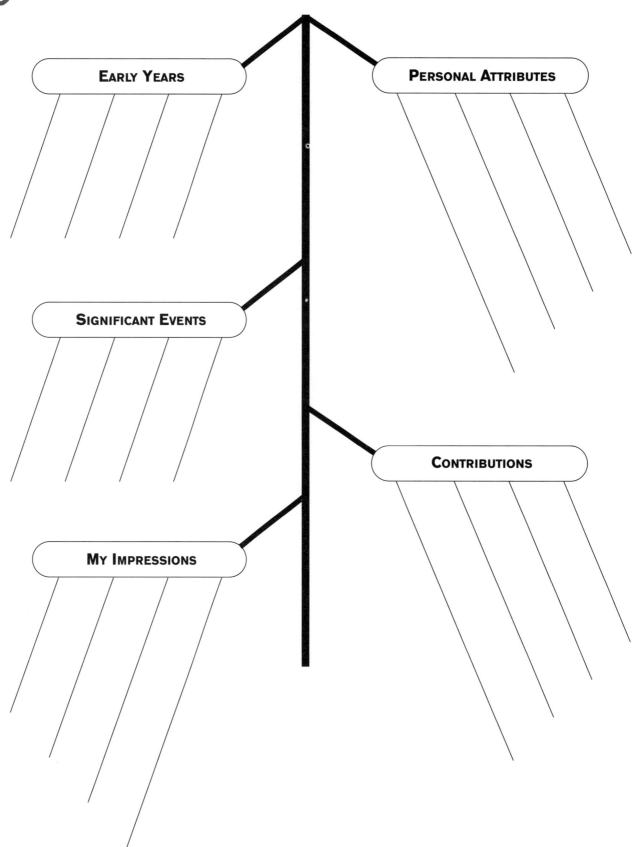

Teaching for Learning Success, Rev. Ed.

GRAPHIC ORGANIZER: SOCIAL STUDIES

INFORMATION ABOUT A COUNTRY OR REGION

NAME OF COUNTRY

GEOGRAPHY

TOPOGRAPHY

CLIMATE

RESOURCES

MAJOR CITIES

OCCUPATIONS

IMPORTS

EXPORTS

GOVERNMENT

CUSTOMS

From *Learning To Learn, Rev. Ed.* by Gloria Frender.
Nashville, TN: Incentive Publications, ©2004. Used by permission.

STUDY SMART VOCABULARY

The "Study Smart Vocabulary" form found on page 250 is a great tool for keeping an organized and thorough list of content-related vocabulary words. The form can serve as a quick reference and study guide for review, providing the student with the most pertinent information for each word. Introduce the form the first time you assign a set of vocabulary words to your students or when you begin a new unit.

Distribute to each student a copy of both the "Study Smart Vocabulary" information sheet on page 249 and the blank form on page 250. Discuss with your students how to use the form with your first vocabulary word as an example.

STUDY SMART VOCABULARY

©2004 by Incentive Publications, Inc., Nashville, TN

Vocabulary Word	Pronunciation	My Definition	Dictionary Definition	Sentence	Related Concepts
1. baleen, p. 113 (dictionary)	bə-lēn'	strainer in mouth used as filter			
2.					
3.					
4.					
5.					
6.					
7.					
8.					
9.					
10.					

250

Teaching for Learning Success, Rev.

STUDY SMART VOCABULARY

WHY

◆ The study smart vocabulary form helps students group all vocabulary words for one subject in one place.

◆ It organizes vocabulary words, definitions, and word usage.

◆ It saves time and effort by eliminating the need to look up the same words again and again.

◆ It provides students with a quick-and-easy study sheet.

HOW

1. When a new vocabulary word is introduced in the textbook or a lecture, copy it onto the "Vocabulary Word" column of your form. For future reference, be sure to write the page number of the book in which you found the word defined or the date of the class in which the word was introduced.

2. Look up the word in the dictionary and write how it is pronounced in the "Pronunciation" column.

3. Read the definition that best fits the use of the word, and then write that definition in your own words in the "My Definition" column.

4. Copy the dictionary's definition in the "Dictionary Definition" column.

5. Copy from the textbook the sentence in which the word was used, or make up your own sentence in the "Sentence" column.

6. Write some related topics, subject areas, or synonyms in the "Related Concepts" column.

Vocabulary Word	Pronunciation	My Definition	Dictionary Definition	Sentence	Related Concepts
baleen, p. 113 (dictionary)	bə-len'	Strainer in mouth used as filter	stiff, flexible substance growing from upper jaw of certain whales	The baleen is used to catch plankton.	humpback whale, fin whale, blue whale

STUDY SMART VOCABULARY

Vocabulary Word	Pronunciation	My Definition	Dictionary Definition	Sentence	Related Concepts
1.					
2.					
3.					
4.					
5.					
6.					
7.					
8.					
9.					
10.					

Teaching for Learning Success, Rev. Ed.

WEEKLY REVIEW

Research reveals that the practice of short daily reviews is a far more successful study strategy than is one long session of cramming at the last minute. Weekly reviews are just as necessary as daily ones and will save students a great deal of effort, time, and stress when the test date draws near.

Discuss the concept of weekly reviews with your students, and convince them to practice this study strategy early in the year or course. A good time to introduce weekly reviews is near the end of a week during which you started a new unit. Distribute to each student copies of the weekly review information sheet found on page 252 and the review worksheet intended for one course found on page 253. It is a good idea to complete the first week's review sheet as a class. You may want to make an overhead transparency of this handout and model how to complete it before asking students to complete their personal copies. Review the students' sheets after the second week to make sure they are completing the form correctly.

The weekly review for all courses (found on page 254) allows students to transfer this strategy to their other classes and is a great parent-pleaser, as it clearly outlines the information students are learning.

WEEKLY REVIEW

WHY

◆ A weekly review helps you keep up with your course work.

◆ It provides a simple format for a weekly overview of course content.

◆ It makes reviewing for quizzes and tests more organized, saving you time.

◆ Writing all of the information in one place improves your memory.

◆ Thinking about and writing the information one more time encourages active learning.

◆ A weekly review reveals any material missing due to a class absence.

◆ It serves as a reminder of areas that need additional review.

◆ It serves as a brief review of information that has already been covered (vocabulary words, main concepts, etc.).

WHEN

◆ At the end of every week, take a few minutes to complete the weekly review chart. You may choose to complete one chart for all classes or one chart for each individual course.

◆ Review this chart briefly each time you begin to study.

◆ Add to this chart daily. Then, review all entries at the end of the week.

WHERE

◆ Keep your weekly review charts in a notebook with class notes and other handouts for that course.

Example

Course Title	Main Topics Covered	New Vocabulary	I Learned:	Questions I Have:
Geology/ Science	rock types	igneous sedimentary metamorphic strata	igneous = volcanic sedimentary = deposited metamorphic = altered by heat	Are fossils only in sedimentary? What's the difference between igneous and metamorphic?

WEEKLY REVIEW

(One Course)

Name _____

Course _____ Dates: _____ /_____ to _____ /_____

	MAIN TOPICS COVERED	NEW VOCABULARY	I LEARNED:	QUESTIONS I HAVE:
week of _____ text pgs. _____ _____ _____				
week of _____ text pgs. _____ _____ _____				
week of _____ text pgs. _____ _____ _____				
week of _____ text pgs. _____ _____ _____				
week of _____ text pgs. _____ _____ _____				
week of _____ text pgs. _____ _____ _____				

WEEKLY REVIEW

(All Courses)

Name _____

Course _____ Dates: _____ / _____ to _____ / _____

COURSE TITLE	MAIN TOPICS COVERED	NEW VOCABULARY	I LEARNED:	QUESTIONS I HAVE:

Teaching for Learning Success, Rev. Ed.

TEST REVIEW SHEETS

The test review sheet on the following page provides an organized format for reviewing for tests and quizzes. This form is helpful to students because it requires them to complete specific information rather than to simply "take notes." In addition to guiding students into a more organized plan of attack for studying, the form illustrates pertinent questions to ask during a review session. Hand a copy of page 256 to every student to fill in whenever you review for a test in class.

Review with students other strategies mentioned in this book that work well when studying for tests, such as "Switch: The Perfect Game" (see pages 287–288) and "Sponges" (see pages 281–283).

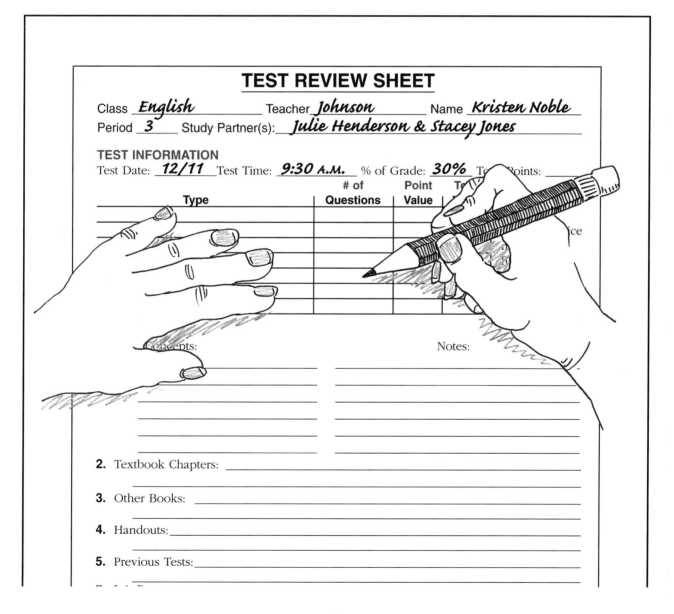

TEST REVIEW SHEET

Class _English_   Teacher _Johnson_   Name _Kristen Noble_
Period _3_   Study Partner(s): _Julie Henderson & Stacey Jones_

TEST INFORMATION
Test Date: _12/11_ Test Time: _9:30 A.M._   % of Grade: _30%_ T... ...oints: _____

Type	# of Questions	Point Value	T...
			...ce

...cepts: Notes:

2. Textbook Chapters: _____

3. Other Books: _____

4. Handouts: _____

5. Previous Tests: _____

TEST REVIEW SHEET

Class _____ Teacher_____ Name _____

Period _____ Study Partner(s):_____

TEST INFORMATION

Test Date: _____Test Time: _____ % of Grade: _____ Total Points: _____

Type	# of Questions	Point Value	Total Value	Types:
_____				true/false
_____				multiple choice
_____				matching
_____				fill-in-blank
_____				essay
_____				open book
_____				take home

CONTENT

1. Main Concepts: Notes:

      _____   _____

      _____   _____

      _____   _____

      _____   _____

      _____   _____

      _____   _____

2. Textbook Chapters: _____

_____

3. Other Books: _____

4. Handouts:_____

_____

5. Previous Tests: _____

6. Lab Reports: _____

7. Vocabulary Words:

    _____   _____   _____

    _____   _____   _____

    _____   _____   _____

    _____   _____   _____

8. Notes:

_____

_____

_____

_____

Teaching for Learning Success, Rev. Ed.

GROUP ACTIVITY REPORTS

Make one copy of the "Group Activity Report Sheet" on page 258 for each student or group. You may also want to make a transparency of the form to display on the overhead projector. This will allow students to watch as you demonstrate how to complete the form (a real plus for visual learners).

Read through the following information before completing the form. Additional space is available on the form to add any specific categories or concepts you wish.

1. **Activity**:
   the name of the project

2. **Goals**:
   description of final student outcome or student product

3. **Time Limit:**
   length of time in which the assignment is to be completed (during the class, by the end of the class, a specific time and date in the future, etc.)

4. **Characteristics of Project:**
   specific details of the assignment

5. **Group Members:**
   the group as a whole lists and rates the members by writing numbers in the boxes that correspond to individual names; or, if each student in the group has a copy of the handout, they may individually rate all members. You can set your own grade distribution for the point system.)

6. **Reporter:**
   student who reports to the teacher for questions and directions (It is always easier to have the group appoint an individual to communicate with the teacher instead of dealing with the entire group.)

7. **Grading:**
   the specific details and points/grades given to each aspect of the activity or project

8.–10. Add your own categories.

GROUP ACTIVITY REPORT SHEET

Recorder's Name _____ Date _____

Class _____ Period _____

  1. Activity: _____

  2. Goals: _____

  3. Time Limit: _____

  4. Characteristics of Project:

      _____   _____

      _____   _____

      _____   _____

      _____

  5. Group Members:

	on-task	cooperative	productive	responsible
_____	____	____	____	____
_____	____	____	____	____
_____	____	____	____	____
_____	____	____	____	____
_____	____	____	____	____
_____	____	____	____	____

1=poor 2=fair 3=good

  6. Reporter: _____

  7. Grading:

      _____   _____

      _____   _____

      _____   _____

      _____   _____

  8. _____

     _____

     _____

  9. _____

     _____

     _____

  10. _____

     _____

     _____

     _____

     _____

SCIENCE LAB REPORTS

Consider the following suggestions to make your science labs more organized and successful.

1. Let students choose their own partners or groups. They tend to work better in groups of their own choosing.

2. Whenever possible, arrange student seats according to lab groups or partners. This type of arrangement makes it much easier to spot groups that did not clean up their work areas.

3. Enforce a policy that requires absent students to get lab data from their partners or group members and write their own conclusions. It is very difficult to repeat a lab experience for one or two students, and most of the time it is not necessary. This policy also encourages good attendance.

Use the science lab report on page 260 to encourage better organization, focused task completion, and better lab results. You may choose to distribute a copy of the form to each student or one to each group. Students can also be directed to complete the report as homework or under teacher supervision while participating in the lab.

Complete the teacher's checklist for lab (form found on page 261) for a quick-and-easy evaluation of students' overall lab achievements. Use simple check marks, points, or grades for each task listed. Depending on class size and time limitations, complete either one form per student or one per group.

SCIENCE LAB REPORT

Name _____ Date _____

Class _____ Period _____ Grade ____

1. Title: _____ Objective/Purpose: _____

2. Materials: _____
   _____
   _____
   _____

3. Pre-lab Questions: _____
   _____
   _____
   _____

4. Key Vocabulary: _____
   _____
   _____
   _____

5. Procedure: _____
   _____
   _____
   _____

6. Data (charts, observations, measurements, etc.):

7. Concluding Questions/Paragraph: _____
   _____
   _____
   _____

8. What did you learn? _____
   _____
   _____
   _____

Teaching for Learning Success, Rev. Ed.

TEACHER'S CHECKLIST FOR LAB

Class _____ Period ____ Date _____

Lab Group _____ Grade _____

_____ 1. Prepared for lab (wore safety equipment, dressed appropriately, assignments completed, etc.)

_____ 2. On-task

_____ 3. Worked well with lab partners

_____ 4. Completed pre-lab report form

_____ 5. Documentation

_____ 6. Recorder: _____

_____ 7. Retrieved/returned materials: _____

_____ 8. Cleaned lab area

_____ 9. Readied lab materials for next class

_____ 10. Anatomy quiz/Dissection

_____ 11. Oral quiz

_____ 12. _____

_____ 13. _____

_____ 14. _____

_____ 15. _____

Comments:

_____

_____

_____

_____

_____

_____

_____

_____

_____

_____

_____

_____

_____

©2004 by Incentive Publications, Inc., Nashville, TN
Acknowledgement of credit is made to Lynn Stephens
for the above material.

MEMORY TIPS

Memorizing information is an integral part of any curriculum. To make memorizing easier, choose memorization methods that work with natural brain functions instead of against them. The ideas on the following pages are based on research that analyzes the best ways to memorize information; they also demonstrate practical applications. Any time you assign material to be memorized, keep these handy techniques in mind, and distribute the hand-outs according to your students' needs.

MEMORY TIP:
Word Links

MATERIALS

- ◆ pen or pencil
- ◆ paper
- ◆ information you are trying to memorize

PROCESS

- ◆ Read through the information you are trying to memorize and group it into pairs, definitions, etc.
- ◆ For each pair, definition, etc., invent a funny story that actually uses the words together or reminds you of the definition.
- ◆ Briefly write out these associations, underline the particular words you are trying to associate, and read the information out loud as you write it.
- ◆ Read the information out loud a second time.
- ◆ Practice saying the stories that link the information at least 2–3 times a day for a period of 2–3 days.

Example

Salem is the capital of **Oregon.**

*"There are many sailboats on the coast of **Oregon** because it is by the ocean. If I lived there I would **"sail 'em."***

MEMORY TIP:
3" x 5" Cards

MATERIALS

- 3" x 5" cards
- pen or pencil
- hole punch
- split ring

PROCESS

- Punch holes in the upper right- or left-hand corner of the cards.

- Write one item on the front of a card. Be sure to hear it, see it, say it, and write it at the same time.

- Write the answer on the back of the card. Be sure to hear it, see it, say it, and write it at the same time.

- Take 3–5 of the cards (one "set") and insert the ring in the holes.

- Quiz yourself. Read aloud the item on the front of the first card and say aloud the matching answer. Flip the card over to check your answer. If it is correct put a check mark at the top of the card.

- Quiz yourself using the other cards.

- Add another set of 3–5 cards behind the first set and repeat all of the above steps.

HINTS

- Quiz yourself on up to 10 cards at one sitting. Leave time between memorizing the information and quizzing yourself.

- The best time to memorize and review is immediately before going to sleep at night.

- When 5 check marks appear at the top of a card, the information is stored in your long-term memory.

- Always review all previous cards before adding new ones.

MEMORY TIP:

Memorizing in Sequence

MATERIALS

- pen or pencil
- paper
- the material you want to learn

PROCESS

- In a column on the left-hand side of your paper, number the steps you follow when completing a particular task, such as getting dressed, setting the table, etc.
- On the right-hand side of the paper, number a column to match the one on the left.
- In sequential order, write one fact from the information you need to learn in the right-hand column for every step in the left-hand column. Each fact should correspond to a step of your daily task.
- Review the columns for accuracy. Are both in the correct order?
- Read the information and, as you read, link the two columns so that each time you complete the task, you automatically think of the facts you must memorize. Work on no more than five steps and facts at one time.
- Physically practice these steps. Complete the steps, one by one, while repeating aloud the matching facts. Repeat these facts every time you complete this particular routine.
- Practice writing down the facts in order as you visualize yourself walking through the task.
- When you need to recall the facts for a test, simply visualize yourself completing the appropriate task and link the facts to the steps in the correct order.

REMEMBER

- Practice 3–5 "action steps" and facts at one time.
- Every time you complete this particular task, repeat aloud the facts in proper sequence.
- Periodically, practice visualizing and writing the facts so this process will seem natural when taking a test.
- Talk to yourself while writing your list. This helps your memory.
- Intend to link your action steps and facts together every time you practice.

Example

"Action Steps"	"Facts"
Setting the Dinner Table	**Presidents of the United States of America**
1. Take out placemats.	1. George Washington
2. Put placemats on the table.	2. John Adams
3. Take out plates.	3. Thomas Jefferson
4. Put plates on placemats.	4. James Madison
5. Take out silverware.	5. James Monroe
6. Place silverware around plates.	6. John Quincy Adams
7. Take out napkins.	7. Andrew Jackson
8. Fold napkins.	8. Martin Van Buren
9. Place napkins next to forks.	9. William Harrison
10. Take out glasses.	10. John Tyler
11. Place glasses on table.	11. James Polk

You can make your "action steps" as detailed as you want depending on how many facts you need to memorize. For example, "taking out silverware" could become "taking out knives," "taking out forks," "taking out spoons," etc.

MEMORY TIP:
Using Acronyms

An acronym is a word formed by the initial letters of a name or series of words.

MATERIALS

♦ pen or pencil

♦ paper

♦ information you want to learn

PROCESS

♦ Make a vertical or horizontal list of the information to be memorized. If it must be in a specific order, be sure it is listed correctly; if it does not have to be in any specific order, try to organize the information in related groups.

♦ Print (in uppercase letters) the first letter of each word or phrase in a vertical or horizontal line.

♦ Using each of the capital letters as the beginning of a new word, make up a word or phrase you will remember.

♦ Talk out loud to yourself throughout this process.

♦ Without looking at the original list, try to reproduce the acronyms in the correct sequence. Then, write in the real words.

♦ Complete the previous step 2–3 times a day for a period of 2–3 days.

Example

The Great Lakes of the United States of America:

H	O	M	E	S
U	N	I	R	U
R	T	C	I	P
O	A	H	E	E
N	R	I		R
	I	G		I
	O	A		O
		N		R

MEMORY TIP:
When in Doubt, Draw It Out

MATERIALS

- pen or pencil
- colored pens or pencils
- paper
- plastic template of shapes
- the information you want to learn or problems you want to solve

PROCESS

1. Read the material once for overall understanding, and then again for the details.

2. Divide the information or problem into appropriate smaller parts or details.

3. Draw a picture that represents the first detail, or draw a graphic organizer using different shapes and colors for each detail, labeling each shape.

4. Proceed to the next detail adding to your picture or graphic organizer.

5. Add to your picture as you reread each section; continue this process until you have completed the information or problem.

Remember

- Understand each part of the drawing, picture, or organizer as you add to it.
- Talk out loud to yourself as you draw.
- When your drawing or organizer is complete, study it for a few minutes, and then reproduce it on another sheet of paper without looking at the original. When you are finished, compare it to the original to make sure it is accurate.
- Try drawing your picture from memory 2–3 times a day for a period of 2–3 days.

Hand-In

Final Draft

Editing

The Writing Process

Thought

Brain-Storming

Rough Draft

I. Main Topic
A.
B.
1.
2.
3.
II.

Outlining

MEMORY TIP:

———— Objects and Action ————

MATERIALS

- ◆ pen or pencil
- ◆ paper
- ◆ information to be learned

PROCESS

- ◆ Read aloud the information to be learned. Divide it into smaller parts by organizing the information into groups of items that share common characteristics.
- ◆ Think of an object that you could use as a central figure, and imagine the information you are trying to learn revolving around that object or doing something active involving that object.
- ◆ Practice saying the information out loud several times while looking at the list of information.
- ◆ Practice saying the information out loud several times without looking at the list of information.
- ◆ Practice picturing the object and saying the information 2–3 times a day for a period of 2–3 days.

Example

Learn the part of speech called prepositions by holding up your finger and listing the action that could take place around that finger. For example: "to, from, away, around, etc."

or

Think of a cat and an empty box in a room. What could the cat do with the box? It could jump in, out, over, or around the box.

MEMORY TIP:
Sing a Song; Say a Verse

MATERIALS

- pen or pencil
- paper

PROCESS

- Write the information you need to learn in the correct sequence or grouping. Talk out loud to yourself as you do this.

- Think of a song you know well. Hum the melody a few times. Try to sing it using the information you wrote as the lyrics. If your lyrics do not match the melody, try another melody. Be sure to sing out loud each time.

or

- Separate the information into short phrases. Put two phrases together so that the end words rhyme.

- Repeat the phrases out loud several times.

- Practice singing the songs or saying the verses out loud 2–3 times a day for a period of 2–3 days.

Hint: Familiar melodies such as "Twinkle, Twinkle Little Star,"
"Mary Had a Little Lamb," and
"Row, Row, Row Your Boat" work well.

Make up short verses such as:
"In fourteen hundred and ninety-two,
Columbus sailed the ocean blue."

MEMORY TIP:

— Make a Tape —

MATERIALS

- pen or pencil
- paper
- information you are trying to learn
- tape recorder
- blank cassette tape

PROCESS

- Write the information to be learned in small units (for example, one vocabulary word and its definition; one Spanish word and its equivalent English word, etc.). Talk aloud as you write.
- Record each unit of information three times, leaving enough time between the units to repeat each word aloud when you replay the tape.
- Complete 3–5 new words, concepts, or phrases, and then rewind the tape and play it back.
- Listen to yourself say the words, and repeat them during the silent portions of the tape. Continue until you have finished your first set of 3–5 words.
- When you have finished the first set, begin the process over with a new set of 3–5 words.

Example

Making the tape:

Say each set of words aloud three times, leaving enough time between each reading to repeat them once.

"gato, cat" (pause) "gato, cat" (pause) "gato, cat" (pause)

"ratón, mouse" (pause) "ratón, mouse" (pause) "ratón, mouse" (pause)

"pájaro, bird" (pause) "pájaro, bird" (pause) "pájaro, bird" (pause)

Playing the tape:

When you replay the tape, repeat the words during your pauses.

MEMORY TIP:
Hookups

MATERIALS

- pen or pencil
- paper
- information you are trying to learn

PROCESS

- In a vertical line on the left-hand side of a piece of paper, write the letters of the alphabet (use uppercase letters). Skip several spaces between each letter.
- Write each key word or phrase of the information you are studying to the right of the letter of the alphabet to which it corresponds. Talk out loud as you write.
- Review one letter at a time by rewriting the information. Talk as you write. Repeat this process twice before reviewing the next letter.
- Learn the information associated with 3–5 letters at one time.
- After studying the first 3–5 letters, take a break or study something else, and then review the information you have already learned.
- Start on another set of 3–5 letters.
- Practice this 2–3 times a day for a period of 2–3 days.

Example

The Fifty United States

$$\mathbf{A} = \begin{matrix} \text{Alabama} \\ \text{Alaska} \\ \text{Arkansas} \end{matrix}$$

GOOD REVIEW QUESTIONS

Do you ever wonder if you really know what you think you know? Do you wonder if you know the material well enough for a quiz, test, or discussion? To find out, ask yourself the following questions. If you can answer all of the questions that apply to the material you are studying, you have thoroughly learned the information.

◆ Can you briefly summarize what you just read?
  What/who was important and why?

◆ Can you explain your answer?

◆ Can you state examples and tell why they are important?

◆ Do you agree? Why or why not?

◆ How did you arrive at your answer or solution?
  What was your thinking process?

◆ What facts support your view, and can you think of
  other facts not stated in your material?

◆ Can you apply these ideas to other situations or information?

◆ Can you add information to this subject or compare
  and contrast it with what you already know?

FUN AND GAMES

✍ *Indicates ready-to-use forms or handouts*

FUN AND GAMES:

An Overview

Positive reinforcement quickly builds positive relationships and strong motivation.

Positive reinforcement and classroom games greatly improve everyone's attitudes. Sharing the fun of learning with students is just as important as sharing knowledge. You will find some great ideas for positive reinforcement throughout the next few pages. Have fun using them in your classroom—this is a good way to get to know your students better.

SUPER STUDENT AWARD

Class _____ Teacher _____ Date _____

____ 1. Great class participation!

____ 2. Excellent class/homework assignment!

____ 3. Very prepared for class today!

____ 4. High grade on quiz/test!

____ 5. Wonderful effort today!

____ 6. Demonstrated great leadership in clas

____ 7. Worked hard on group participation!

____ 8. Demonstrated great cooperation!

____ 9. Diligent and on-task!

____ 10. Extra helpful in class today!

____ 11. _____

____ 12. _____

Comments:
_____
_____
_____

Parent/Guardian Comments:
_____
_____
_____

Honor Award

★ ★ ★ ★ ★

to:
Jessica Hirschbrunner

for:
a helping hand to new students
_____

HONOR AWARD

Here is a terrific reward for every member of your class! Catch your students doing something positive, and let them know that everyone appreciates their efforts. Whether an exceptional project or assignment, a courteous and thoughtful gesture or act, or a helping hand, it deserves recognition.

At the beginning of the school year, request that your students provide you with individual photographs. These will come in handy when posting student awards in the classroom.

Reproduce the master award form on the following page onto brightly colored paper. Make plenty of copies to send home with students throughout the school year. You may also want to enlarge a copy of the form for each of your classes. Laminate these large award forms or cover them with clear contact paper, and post them in prominent places in your classrooms. Use this large award form to post photographs of students who merit recognition. Write the student's name and a brief description of his or her good deed in the spaces provided, and tape the student's photograph in the blank space. Use a transparency pen to write on these large posters. When recognizing a different student on the award form, wipe off the previous student's information with a damp paper towel, and give that student an individual copy of the award to take home.

Keep a record of recipients, and try to include every student during the course or year. Update photos when necessary.

Options

- ◆ Each time a student receives the award, he or she earns extra credit points.

- ◆ Feature a new student each week.

- ◆ Feature a new student at any time.

- ◆ Award a special prize at the end of the school year to the student who earned the most honor awards.

Teaching for Learning Success, Rev. Ed.

Honor Award

to:

_____

for:

_____

_____

_____

Signed _____

DATE:

Teaching for Learning Success, Rev. Ed.

©2004 by Incentive Publications, Inc., Nashville, TN.
Acknowledgement of credit is made to
Carolyn M. Lazar-Kronke for the above material.

SUPER STUDENT AWARD

Class _____ Teacher _____ Date _____

____ 1. Great class participation!

____ 2. Excellent class/homework assignment!

____ 3. Very prepared for class today!

____ 4. High grade on quiz/test!

____ 5. Wonderful effort today!

____ 6. Demonstrated great leadership in class!

____ 7. Worked hard on group participation!

____ 8. Demonstrated great cooperation!

____ 9. Diligent and on-task!

____ 10. Extra helpful in class today!

____ 11. _____

____ 12. _____

Comments: _____

_____

_____

_____

_____

Parent/Guardian Comments: _____

_____

_____

_____

_____

_____   _____
Teacher Signature   Parent/Guardian Signature

©2004 by Incentive Publications, Inc., Nashville, TN.
Acknowledgement of credit is made to
Carolyn M. Lazar-Kronke for the above material.

Teaching for Learning Success, Rev. Ed.

SPONGES

WHAT

- ◆ A sponge is a name for any short activity (usually not exceeding 5 minutes).

- ◆ A sponge activity is given to the entire class, usually at the beginning of the period.

- ◆ A sponge activity can incorporate a wide variety of materials.

- ◆ A sponge activity can be used to introduce a topic to the class.

- ◆ A sponge activity need not be entirely related to class content.

WHY

- ◆ A sponge activity encourages students' interest in a subject and focuses their attention.

- ◆ A sponge activity is fun.

- ◆ Completing a sponge activity creates enthusiasm for a subject.

- ◆ It generates positive student excitement.

- ◆ It provides a non-threatening learning atmosphere and encourages risk-taking.

- ◆ It involves everyone in the class—even those students who rarely perform get "hooked."

- ◆ A sponge activity sets a positive tone at the beginning of class.

- ◆ It is a quiet student activity, good to issue while you take attendance.

- ◆ It can serve as a review or quick pretest.

- ◆ Completing a sponge activity strengthens problem-solving and higher-level thinking skills (depending on material chosen for the sponge).

- ◆ It encourages students to arrive on time for your class.

MATERIALS

- ◆ chalkboard or dry-erase board

- ◆ transparencies and an overhead projector (preferable to the chalkboard/dry-erase board because they can be reused year after year and require less preparation than writing the information on the board)

- ◆ a variety of content-related activities able to be completed within 5 minutes, such as:
  - • 3–5 content questions or vocabulary definitions from the previous day's class (one-word, short-phrase answers)

SPONGES

- 3–5 content questions or vocabulary definitions from new material to be covered in today's class
- word puzzles
- short logic problems
- word games
- math, science, history, language arts puzzles

You can find books containing these types of activities at many educational supply stores or through educational supply catalogs, at book stores, drug and grocery stores, on restaurant placemats, in newspapers, and magazines.

HOW

1. Collect a wide variety of materials directly related to your subject area.

   Include some unrelated materials just for fun.

2. Write the number of sponge items on the board during a free period or first thing in the morning.

   or

3. Make transparencies from these materials.

   Label a file folder "Sponges" and keep all transparencies ready for immediate use.

4. Have the activity ready when students walk in your classroom.

   They may begin at that time or as soon as the bell rings or class starts.

5. Instruct each student to take a slip of paper or a piece of scratch paper from the potpourri table and write his or her name on it.

6. You may instruct students to complete the sponge activity by themselves, in pairs, or in groups for individual or shared credit.

7. While students are completing the sponge activity, you can take attendance, distribute handouts, review lesson plans, etc.

Teaching for Learning Success, Rev. Ed.

8. Stop the activity after 5 minutes, and ask students to exchange and correct the papers.

9. You may choose to give students points to be applied to extra credit or a future assignment, or give an all-or-nothing grade for the sponge activity itself. To save time, consider collecting only those papers with points.

10. If you choose to use sponges every day, students may accrue a large amount of points.

    If so, you may want to make a chart to show that a certain amount of sponge activity points must be earned for every point of extra credit. Total the points periodically, convert them according to your scale, and add them to your gradebook.

Have fun with this activity! It is a big hit with everyone!

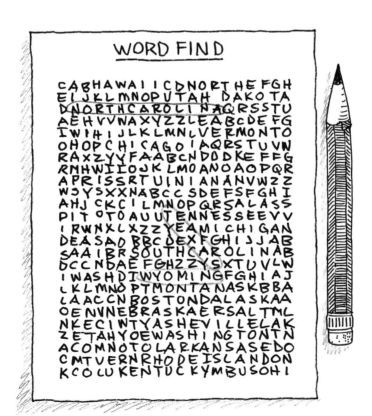

CREATIVE ATTENTION GRABBERS

Are you looking for an activity that grabs your students' attention, stimulates their curiosity, and makes your class more interesting? Try a few of the following ideas as class starters.

1. Place a phone in one of your desk drawers and make a tape recording of a telephone ringing.

   As students are coming into class, turn on the tape recorder. (Time the telephone ring to start as soon as all students are seated.) Answer the phone and carry on a one-sided conversation that introduces your topic of study. Mention a student's name now and then in the course of your conversation.

2. When class begins, don't say a word.

   Use pantomime to introduce the day's activity or subject. Each time a student correctly guesses the information you are presenting, write it on the board. Continue until the students discover the topic.

   Variations:

   ◆ In the following days, appoint or ask for student volunteers to do the same. Write the topic, key vocabulary word, etc., on a slip of paper and hand it to the student who will pantomime the activity for the rest of the class.

   ◆ Ask another teacher to enter your room at the beginning of class and pantomime the topic.

3. Play a game of hangman with vocabulary words introduced the day before.

4. Draw on the chalkboard a horizontal line that is intersected by a vertical line, thus forming four quadrants of equal size.

   In the upper left-hand quadrant, draw a "+" (plus) sign. In the upper right-hand quadrant, draw a "–" (minus) sign. Choose a concept that will be taught in class today or one introduced during a previous class. In the lower left-hand quadrant, write a synonym for the concept. In the lower right-hand quadrant, write an antonym for the concept. Do not tell the students anything about the words or the symbols. Ask students to come up with some words related to information you have been studying. It is only a matter of time before a student mentions a

Teaching for Learning Success, Rev. Ed.

word that should be included in one of the columns (either an antonym or a synonym of the concept). When the lists of clues become long enough, ask the students to guess the concept. After students understand the rules of this game, write only one word in either of the columns.

5. Wear a costume or mask.

6. Arrange a mock interview with another teacher, an administrator, the daytime janitor, or anyone else available.

   Write interview questions on index cards, and ask your guest to read the questions to you. These cards should contain leading (and hopefully humorous) questions about your personal experiences with the content material to be introduced during the class period. For example, you may decide to invent a tale in which your use or application of the concept came to your rescue, saved your life, made you rich, etc. The more outlandish your story is, the more students will enjoy it.

7. Spell out a phrase, short sentence, or key vocabulary word related to the day's topic on 5" x 8" index cards, writing one letter on each card.

   Shuffle the cards and give one card to each student. When class begins, provide a minimum number of clues and directions, and ask the students to arrange the letters to compose the required word, phrase, or sentence.

8. As students are entering the classroom, stand in the doorway with a role of toilet tissue and instruct each student to take as many sheets as he or she wishes.

   When class begins, instruct all students to pile their tissue sheets on the tops of their desks. For each piece of tissue on their desks, the students must stand up and repeat something learned during the previous day's (or week's) class. Do not let students repeat information.

9. Play a game of "20 Questions."

   In an attempt to guess the day's topic, students ask questions to which you answer only "yes" or "no."

10. Use a code to write on the chalkboard the concept, vocabulary word, or phrase to be introduced. Students work in small groups to solve the mystery.

"I'M DONE! NOW WHAT?"

This project is easy to make, simple to maintain and store, and useable for many years to come. Students find it fun and motivating as it offers a great deal of variety and is not complicated.

MATERIALS

- ◆ enrichment activity or game and puzzle books appropriate to grade level
- ◆ box with separate lid (large enough in which to store the books)
- ◆ plastic report covers or clear contact paper
- ◆ overhead transparency pens
- ◆ strapping tape
- ◆ contact paper to cover box (optional)

PROCESS

1. Tear the pages from a paperback book of crossword puzzles, word searches, word games, mazes, pencil or pen game books, hidden picture puzzles, logic problems, etc. These books can be found in educational supply stores, book stores, and grocery stores.

2. Place each page in a clear plastic report cover or cover it with clear contact paper. Cover the answer keys with plastic as well.

3. Stand the pages in a box. If you store several different books in the same box, use a labeled file folder to separate them, and color code all of the pages and their answer keys.

4. Attach the front cover(s) of the book(s) to the outside of the box for easy identification.

5. Supply overhead transparency pens. Students should use the transparency pens to write their answers on the plastic-covered pages.

6. After completion, students use a damp paper towel to erase their answers.

Teaching for Learning Success, Rev. Ed.

SWITCH:
The Perfect Game

This game has met with overwhelming success in every content area and with grades ranging from third to twelfth!

BENEFITS

◆ This game encourages the involvement of every student in a team activity.

◆ It is a non-threatening motivational game.

◆ Flexible variations allow for many uses throughout the school year.

USES

◆ Homework Starter: Using "Switch" as a homework starter gives everyone a head start on a homework assignment by supplying a few of the answers. This tactic encourages even the most reluctant student to begin the assignment!

◆ Pretest: This is a perfect format with which to test class knowledge of the subject area to be introduced. You may want to divide the class into teams. The team with the highest number of correct answers wins the game.

◆ Review: Use the game to review material before a test, quiz, or class discussion. Allow students to keep their papers at the end of the game. You may want to allow students to use additional class time to complete their papers, working either individually or in teams.

◆ Class Discussion: Use the game to introduce topics and ideas that spark class discussion.

◆ Time Filler: Play this game to fill any extra time you have on your hands, whether it be because you find yourself with an extra 5 or 10 minutes at the end of class, you want to reward students for their hard work, your voice is fading, you have a headache, etc.

MATERIALS

◆ Choose handouts that have clear, simple directions. Students must be able to read and comprehend them easily since you do not read or discuss them.

◆ The handout's format should be easy to correct: matching, true/false, one word answers, multiple choice, etc.

◆ Occasionally introduce topics that have nothing to do with the subject you are studying: mazes, crossword puzzles, and word games are fun for students to complete.

SWITCH

To Begin

1. Form students into teams of 3–7 players.

2. Each student needs a writing surface and a pen or pencil.

3. Read or explain the game's rules.

4. Distribute one handout to each student.

5. Begin the game.

Game Rules (Make sure all students understand the rules before handing out papers.)

1. After all handouts are distributed and the teacher says "Go," students may begin to complete their papers.

2. Students should not put their name on their paper.

3. When the teacher says "SWITCH," each student hands his or her paper to a teammate (the person to the left, right, back, or front).

4. There is to be no talking during the game. The penalty for talking is the removal of that student's paper from the game. This action does not stop that student from participating in the game but decreases his or her teammates' chances of winning.

5. Answers may be changed at any time.

6. When a student completes his or her paper and raises his or her hand, the teacher corrects it. The first team who turns on a correctly completed paper wins the game.

7. If the paper is not completed correctly, the teacher will keep the paper, and all teams continue to play. The student is not out of the game, but his or her team is minus one paper.

Review the rules with students, ask for questions, and begin the game.

Variations

◆ Require only a certain number of items to be correct instead of all of the items.

◆ If a question has the entire class confused, give your students verbal or written hints.

CONTENT JEOPARDY

WHAT

◆ Content Jeopardy is a highly motivating game that reviews multiple concepts in any content area.

WHY

◆ The game is fun for all students.

◆ It is a highly motivating activity.

◆ It is a great teaching tool that involves all students.

◆ The game requires students to use library research skills.

◆ It is a great instrument for review.

MATERIALS

◆ chalkboard or dry-erase board to record team scores

◆ thick posterboard, foamboard, or cardboard (must be able to lean against chalkboard or dry-erase board tray without bending), approximately 35" x 50" or larger

◆ yardstick

◆ 25 used library book pockets or small sturdy manila envelopes cut in half to form pockets for 3" x 5" cards

◆ 125 lined or unlined index cards (3" x 5")

◆ 5 brads

◆ 3 index cards (5" x 8") cut into $2\frac{1}{2}$" x 8" strips

◆ single hole punch (to punch a hole in the top center of all $2\frac{1}{2}$" x 8" strips)

◆ felt-tip markers (broad tip)

◆ pencil

◆ rubber cement

◆ team buzzers (optional)

CONTENT JEOPARDY

Constructing the Game Board

Refer to the layout on page 293 as you construct this board.

1. Select sturdy colored posterboard or foamboard, or cover thick cardboard with contact paper.

2. Cut the 5" x 8" index cards into strips of 2½" x 8" each. These will serve as the category title cards.

3. Along the top of the game board, mark in pencil 5 columns of equal size, leaving space for margins on the left- and right-hand side of the board.

4. Mark the middle of each column approximately 2" from the top. Punch a hole in the top center of each of the 2½" x 8" category cards. Place each of the five category cards in a column along the top of the game board. Use brads to secure the cards to the board. Write a category title on each of the cards.

5. Leaving a 2" space along the bottom of the board, evenly distribute 25 library book pockets or manila envelopes into the 5 columns.

6. On the front of each pocket, write the point value from 1 to 5 in ascending order (1 at the top of the column, 5 at the bottom).

Student Preparation

1. Show students the game board and explain to them the rules for play.

2. Have students brainstorm 5 category titles related to your current unit of study. (For example, in a Language Arts/Literature unit, your categories could be Genre, Authors, Book Titles, Time Period, and Potpourri.)

3. Divide the class into 5 groups (either assigned or self-selected).

4. Assign or have students choose one category title per group.

5. Distribute to each student the same number of index cards (3" x 5").

6. As a team, students will research their topics in the library or media center. Inform the teams that each student is responsible for creating 5 questions (one for each level of difficulty) related to his or her category. Questions worth 1 point should be the easiest to answer and those worth 5 points should be the most difficult to answer. No duplicate questions are allowed.

7. On one side of the card write "Q-1" in the upper left-hand corner. This shows that this is the question side of the card and is worth one point. Write the the question in

the middle of the card. On the other side of the card, write the question's answer. Write "A-1" in the upper left-hand corner of this side of the card.

8. Each student should write his or her name and the amount of points the question is worth on the answer side of the card that he or she created. During the game, the student who wrote the question is not eligible to play when his or her card is read. If a student tries to answer a card that he or she created, his or her team loses the number of points assigned that card.

9. Clearly explain your expectations and assign grade points per card for this assignment as you see fit. You may decide to assign individual grades or a group grade. Students are required to write their names on the answer side of each card, so you will be able to assess the number of cards and the quality of work each student turns in.

10. Students hand in cards by category. (Place a rubber band around each set of cards to keep them organized.)

Teacher Preparation

1. Before placing the question and answer cards in their corresponding pockets, you will need to:

   ◆ review the cards and assign grade points for each student, if you wish.

   ◆ review cards for accurate format and information, as well as any duplicates.

   ◆ assess whether each question matches its designated level of difficulty.

2. Place the question cards in the pockets so that the answer side and assigned points are visible.

3. You are ready to play.

4. To use again, simply make new category and question and answer cards.

5. When you are ready to play the game again using different categories:

   a. remove the category cards.

   b. remove the 3" x 5" question and answer cards (group them by category).

   c. place all of the materials in a manila envelope labeled "Content Jeopardy." List all of the categories on the outside of the folder for easy reference.

CONTENT JEOPARDY

Content Jeopardy Rules

1. Form 3–5 teams.

2. Each team chooses a captain who is responsible for:

   ◆ selecting the category and point value for each play.

   ◆ calling out the team's response.

3. The first team starts the game by selecting a category and point value. For example, the captain of Team 1 might request, "Authors for 3."

4. The teacher selects the chosen card and reads the answer and the name of the student who wrote the card. (That student may not participate in this turn.)

5. All players must wait until the entire answer and student name have been read aloud before responding with the answer's matching question. For a response to be considered correct, the response must be phrased in the form of a question.

6. After the card has been read, the first team captain to raise his or her hand, or press the buzzer, may respond. Team members may work together to come up with the correct question, but only the captain may ask the question.

7. Decide on a time limit for responses. If one team fails to respond within the designated time limit, the other teams can take turns responding.

8. Once the correct question has been given, that team's points are recorded on the board, and the team captain chooses another question.

9. Teams play until class ends, there are no cards left in the pockets, or a predetermined time or amount of points has been reached.

10. Reward all players. Team captains list their team members and the total number of points their teams accumulated. Each team member should receive that number of extra credit points or any other award.

Teaching for Learning Success, Rev. Ed.

CONTENT JEOPARDY GAME BOARD

SAMPLE

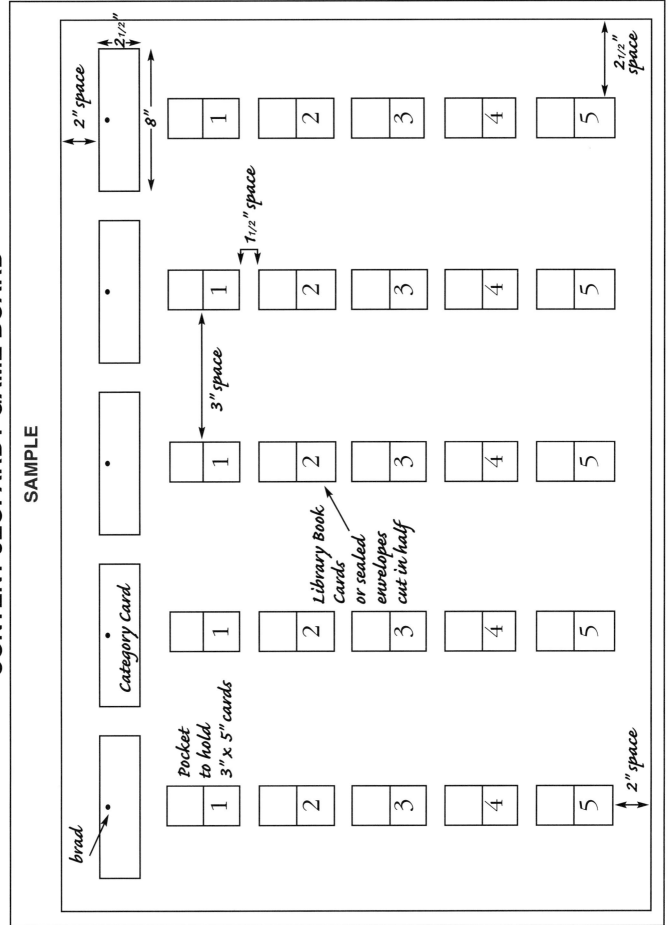

brad

Pocket to hold 3" x 5" cards

Category Card

Library Book Cards or sealed envelopes cut in half

2½"

2" space

8"

1½" space

3" space

2½" space

2" space

CONTENT JEOPARDY QUESTION/ANSWER CARDS

ANSWER CARD

A-3

Hemingway wrote this book about an old fisherman and a young boy.

Kim Johnston

QUESTION CARD

Q-3

What is _The Old Man and The Sea?_

REFERENCES

Cummings, C. *Plan To Teach*. Edmonds, WA: Teaching Inc., 1987. *(Grades 1–12)*
A plan book containing specific, brief weekly teaching tips and quotes.

Epstein, J., Jackson, V., and Salinas, K., editors. *TIPS (Teachers Involve Parents in Schoolwork): A Manual for Teachers*. The Center on Families, Communities, Schools, and Children's Learning. Baltimore, MD: The Johns Hopkins University, 1992. *(Grades 1–7)*
This manual contains materials that incorporate across-the-curriculum concepts into homework assignments that greatly encourage parental involvement. Many of the assignments are open-ended and foster higher-level thinking skills.

Forte, I., Schurr, S. *The Definitive Middle School Guide: A Handbook For Success*. Nashville, TN: Incentive Publications, 1993. *(Grades 5–8)*
This hands-on resource for middle school teachers and administrators provides comprehensive materials and lists in the areas of interdisciplinary teaming, advisory programs, cooperative learning, creative and critical thinking skills, assessment, interdisciplinary instruction, and more.

Forte, I. *Teachers' Treasury*. Nashville, TN: Incentive Publications, 1990. *(Grades 3–6)*
Perfect for unplanned moments or as a supplement to lesson plans, this resource provides language arts, science, math, social studies, art, music, and enrichment activities.

Forte, I. *Teacher-Tested Timesavers*. Nashville, TN: Incentive Publications, 1990. *(Grades K–6)*
This book provides ready-to-reproduce-and-use materials including awards, certificates, patterns, charts, forms, reports, outline maps, math grids, and more.

Frender, G. *Learning to Learn: Strengthening Study Skills and Brain Power, Revised Edition*. Nashville, TN: Incentive Publications, 2004. *(All Levels)* This reference tool introduces practical study skills for success in school and life: ready-to-reproduce-and-use materials in the areas of note taking, organizational skills, test taking, memory skills, power reading, problem solving, time management, memory, and more.

Hammond, D., Lester, T., and Scales, J. *Plexers: A Collection of Word Puzzles* and *More Plexers: A Collection of Word Puzzles*. Palo Alto, CA: Dale Seymour Publications, 1988. *(Grades 4 and up)*
This book introduces a variety activities that promote thinking and language skills. Great resource of ideas for sponge activities. Each word puzzle is a pictorial code for a common phrase, idiomatic expression, or name of a person, place, or thing.

Sebranek, P., Meyer, V., and Kemper, D. *Write Source 2000: A Guide to Writing, Thinking, and Learning*. Burlington, WI: Write Source Educational Publishing House, 1990. *(Grades 3–8)*
Invaluable desktop reference for teachers, students, and parents that stresses the fundamental principals of writing, reading, and thinking. It includes useful tables, lists, maps, math and computer skills, and historical documents.

Sebranek, P., Meyer, V., and Kemper, D. *Writers, Inc*. Burlington, WI: Write Source Educational Publishing House, 1990. *(Grades 9 and up)*
Desktop reference for teachers, students, and parents that stresses the fundamental principals of writing, reading, and thinking. It includes useful tables, lists, maps, math and computer skills, and historical documents.

Yellow Pages Series (7 books). Nashville, TN: Incentive Publications, Inc. *(Grades 2–8)*
Across-the-curriculum reference books containing facts, lists, definitions, charts, and more in the areas of reading, writing, math, science, ecology, and United States and world social studies.